The Dyslexia Handbook 2005

A compendium of articles, checklists, resources and contacts for dyslexic people, their families and teachers. The Dyslexia Handbook is substantially updated and revised each year.

Edited by
Susan Tresman and Ann Cooke

Managing Editor
Kate Vose

Published by
The British Dyslexia Association

Editorial note

The views expressed in this book are those of the individual contributors, and do not necessarily represent the policy of the British Dyslexia Assocation.

The BDA does not endorse the advertisements included in this publication.

Whilst every effort has been made to ensure the accuracy of information given in this handbook, the BDA cannot accept responsibility for the consequences of any errors or omissions in that information.

In certain articles the masculine pronoun is used purely for the sake of convenience.

British Dyslexia Association
The Dyslexia Handbook 2005
1. Great Britain. Education
I. Title II. Susan Tresman & Ann Cooke
ISBN 1-872653-37-5

Published in Great Britain 2005

Designed and typeset by FiSH Books, London
Printed by Almac Book Production Services Limited
1a Barbon Close, London WC1N 3JX
Tel: 020 7405 5607
Fax: 020 7404 8743
Email: almacbps@aol.com

Advertising sales by Space Marketing
Tel: 01892 677740
Fax: 01892 677743
Email: brians@spacemarketing.co.uk

The British Dyslexia Association
98 London Road, Reading RG1 5AU
Telephone: 0118 966 2677
Helpline: 0118 966 8271
Fax: 0118 935 1927
Email: Helpline: info@dyslexiahelp-bda.demon.co.uk
Administration: admin@bda-dyslexia.demon.co.uk
Website: http://www.bda-dyslexia.org.uk/

Registered Charity Number: 289243
Registered in England no. 1830587

Contents

OTHER DYSLEXIA ORGANISATIONS:

Part 2 – Managing Dyslexia in Children and Young People

Part 5 – ICT

Chairman's Foreword

Rodney Clark OBE, Chairman of the BDA

It is immensely gratifying as Chairman to be able to report some of the significant steps that have been taken in 2004. We have continued towards the BDA's vision of a dyslexia friendly society that will enhance the quality of life for all dyslexic people.

New and important partnerships continue to be forged which widen the charity's scope and influence, alongside growth and development within the organisation and in the regions.

Globally, the BDA's information-packed and accessible website attracts vast numbers of visitors many of whom attended our 6th International Conference at Warwick University in the spring. With almost 900 delegates from 35 countries and an impressive team of presenters, the conference highlighted the progress that has been made in the field of dyslexia research and the consequent development in policy and practice. This hugely successful conference reflected the charity's international status and reputation and was a credit to the dedication and skill of the team of volunteers and staff who planned and administered it.

Mainstream activities have also been successful with each of the BDA's three main campaign areas – education, young people in the criminal justice system, and employability – having reached significant milestones in their progress.

In the **education** arena, I am pleased to report that discussion over a period of time with a number of local education authorities has culminated in the production of a unique BDA Quality Mark for LEAs. This is an enormously exciting breakthrough that will raise awareness and standards and gradually increase the number of LEAs and schools conforming to recognised dyslexia friendly criteria. A message of hope and expectation for future generations of dyslexic children.

Following the completion of a pioneering project in Bradford relating to **young people in the criminal justice system,** a successful application for European funding has enabled a collaborative three-year project with NACRO (National Association for the Care and Resettlement of Offenders). This partnership will not only support the rehabilitation of a large group of young prisoners but also build up the BDA's expertise in this area where dyslexic young people are so disproportionately represented. This work represents a landmark in research and will give much needed guidance in this little understood area.

With regard to **employability:** having raised awareness of dyslexia in the workplace over two years with the dyslexia-wise campaign, the BDA this year invited employers to four regional learning networks around the country. Sponsored by Sundial, these interactive networks culminated in the material for a BDA Guide to Employers. This is a major breakthrough in the workplace. We hope it will lead to a working environment where the talents of dyslexic people can flourish and contribute the flair and imagination so valuable to industry and commerce and exhibited by many well-known dyslexic entrepreneurs.

The title of this year's Dyslexia Awareness Week reflected a focus on the talents of dyslexic people, and the tremendous value added to the charity's activities by collaborative working. "Positive about Dyslexia – Partnership in Action" encapsulated the BDA's attitude towards its work as the voice of dyslexic people. While continuing to press for the support necessary to allow dyslexics to reach their potential, we recognise the particular, often unique strengths of many dyslexic people of all ages. Working with others in partnerships helps the BDA to achieve optimum effectiveness in all aspects of its work as evidenced by the impressive campaign results outlined above.

Two new collaborative initiatives to look out for in the year ahead are:

- A Specific Learning Difficulties Forum, initiated by the BDA to explore the common ground and areas of joint action with other SpLD organsations.
- Xtraordinary People, an organisation of talented dyslexic people committed to raising funds through the BDA to make a substantial and positive impact on education and dyslexia. The project is to be launched in late 2004.

With a constituency of five million people in the UK – 10 percent of the population – the association takes its role seriously and looks forward to future challenges and successes with confidence and enthusiasm.

Editors' Introduction

Ann Cooke and Susan Tresman

2004 has been an action packed year for all those involved with the BDA. A new editorial team, Ann Cooke and Susan Tresman, takes up the helm of the BDA Handbook and we hope that you enjoy the new, more colourful, look for this issue. We both feel that the Handbook holds a very important place in communicating key issues about the world of dyslexia to a varied and substantial audience.

The 6th BDA International Conference entitled Dyslexia: The Dividends from Research to Practice took place at the University of Warwick in March. Chaired by Dr Angela Fawcett, it was attended by almost 900 delegates. Judging by the excellent feedback most found it to be of great value and a stimulating and lively event. We are very pleased to have benefited from the views of so many that participated in the conference. Our thanks are extended to Angela, our most able and committed Chair and to the Steering Group for their extensive contribution to ensuring such a memorable occasion. Read all about it in Angela Fawcett and Lindsay Peer's summary of those action packed four days on pages 51–54.

You won't be surprised to learn that our attentions are already directed towards the 7th BDA International Conference! Look out for more news on the BDA website shortly.

In this edition of the Handbook we have again been fortunate in collecting together a series of excellent articles dealing with key issues around supporting dyslexia, enriching the school curriculum, managing dyslexia for children and adults, policy developments and ICT.

Our thanks to Kate Vose, Managing Editor, whose central role in co-ordinating the creation of the Handbook cannot be overstated! We welcome all contributions from new and experienced authors and friends and thank them for their support.

And just to add from Susan how much she is also relishing the new opportunities, achievements and objectives of her role as BDA Education Director. How rapidly the first year in post is slipping by... it must be true that time flies when one is enjoying oneself!

Please enjoy reading this edition and let us know what you think – it's your Handbook.

Part 1

The British Dyslexia Association and Others

The BDA Vision

For the BDA to campaign to break down barriers to inclusion and provide a dyslexia friendly society that enables dyslexic people to reach their potential. It will, with others, provide comprehensive support for an all-age dyslexic population. By the year 2010 we want to see services that enhance the quality of life for all dyslexic people in all communities.

Agreed by the BDA Management Board – October 2001

What is Dyslexia?

Susan Tresman, Chief Executive and BDA Education Director

Peruse ten different publications about dyslexia and you will come across ten different definitions. Here is the BDA's version which we feel best describes dyslexia.

> Dyslexia is a combination of abilities and difficulties that affect the learning process in one or more of reading, spelling, writing and sometimes numeracy. It is a persistent condition. Accompanying weaknesses may be identified in areas of speed of processing, short-term memory, organisation, sequencing, spoken language and motor skills. There may be difficulties with auditory and/or visual perception. It is particularly related to mastering and using written language, which may include alphabetic, numeric and musical notation.
>
> Dyslexia can occur despite normal intellectual ability and teaching. It is constitutional in origin, part of one's make-up and independent of socio-economic or language background.
>
> Some learners have very well developed creative skills and interpersonal skills, others have strong oral skills. Some have no outstanding talents. All have strengths.

Further Information

Handy Hints for Educators Working with Pre-School Aged Children

www.bda-dyslexia.org.uk/main/information/education/t00.asp

Handy Hints for Primary School Teachers

www.bda-dyslexia.org.uk/main/information/education/t01.asp

Handy Hints for Secondary School Teachers

www.bda-dyslexia.org.uk/main/information/education/t02.asp

How Do I Know if I am Dyslexic?

www.bda-dyslexia.org.uk/main/information/adults/a02how.asp

Adult Checklist (compiled by Michael Vinegrad)
www.bda-dyslexia.org.uk/main/information/adults/a03check.asp

Outreach Work in the BDA

Steve Alexander, Former BDA Chief Executive

Just over a year ago the BDA was awarded a significant grant from the Community Fund to support the regional development of the Association. This enabled the charity to recruit six workers operating in England, Wales, and Northern Ireland.

In addition, the charity has three successful national campaigns in the areas of education, offending and employability. Each campaign is informed by regionally based project work and this, combined with regional development, constitutes the BDA's 'outreach work'.

In this article a number of our Regional Development Officers provide a brief glimpse of their work. Project Workers, Helen Boden and Carmel Arnold, also give their impressions.

Regional Development Work in Northern Ireland

Brian Wilson, Regional Development Officer

This past year has presented exciting opportunities for BDA activity in Northern Ireland (NI) with more groups affiliating and new ones starting. There has been significant demand across the Province to create localised support for both parents and adults.

At the time of writing the Local Government Assembly has been suspended due to the faltering peace process. This has resulted in recommendations made in 2002 by a local Government Task Force on Dyslexia not being implemented and the only prospect for the Special Educational Needs Disability Act (SENDA) to be brought in is via emergency legislation.

Despite this there have been excellent opportunities for the BDA to develop partnerships. Work is currently taking place with the five Education & Library Boards (eqivalent of LEAs) and the Education and Training Inspectorate to promote dyslexia friendly schools. In addition work is taking place in the further and higher education sectors with the prospect of our second largest FE College in Londonderry participating in a pilot similar to dyslexia friendly schools. A major project has been funded by the Probation Board in Northern Ireland to work with offenders in North & West Belfast – the areas worst affected by the political conflict. This project involves awareness-raising with Probation Officers and screening and tuition for clients.

Doors have also opened within the construction industry and the NI Civil Service for awareness raising around issues with dyslexia in the workplace. The key focus, however, remains on continuing to build strong local dyslexia associations to provide much needed support and to ensure that the voices of children, parents and dyslexic adults can be heard by our policy makers. We look forward to achieving significant milestones in the coming year.

Regional Development in the North

Pam Varley, Regional Development Officer

Toward the end of last year meetings took place with Darlington & District Dyslexia Support Group and Middlesbrough Support Group. We now have a successful joining together, with Middlesbrough becoming a branch of the Darlington group.

Following regional meetings I produced an adult booklet on needs and provisions. This has proved to be a helpful starting point for what adults may need.

I have been very lucky to be on the steering group for New Dyslexia Visions, which is an exciting project in the West Yorkshire region for 16+ learners and adults. The aims of the group are to provide help and support for adults. Under BDA Project Worker, Helen Boden's, direction I have watched it successfully grow and meet the needs of some of our most vulnerable adults. It gives help about awareness and provides practical support to students in this area.

The Dyslexia Friendly Schools project is proving to be very successful in this region with more and more LEAs looking at ways to address the learning differences of children. Local associations are working extremely hard in this area and my congratulations to those who have achieved success and also to those who are still working towards becoming successful and helping their LEA see the enormous benefits of achieving dyslexia friendly schools.

On a final note, it is inspirational to work with so many dedicated people, both in the voluntary and paid sector, whose main objective is to improve the help and services available for all dyslexic people, young and old.

Regional Development Work in the South West

Ali Bazeley, Regional Development Officer

I have been in post for just over a year and I am gradually getting a good overall view of my area and the local associations. I have found certain patterns emerging, such as an increase in enquiries from adults on the helplines. When I first looked at adult groups and whether associations wanted to set one up, it appeared that there was no demand. However, in the last six months a lot of helpliners have noticed the increase in enquiries from adults. I am now contacting some callers to see if they would like to be involved in setting up adult support groups. In counties where the association is helping with Adult Basic Skills training I am also meeting those groups to see if they too would like to get involved.

In another county I have been talking with the local Parent Partnership Scheme who want to run courses for parents to help them help their children with their homework. They hope to deliver this training through the SENCOs, with help from the local association. Again, I am going along to the meetings to see if I can help start up satellite groups in the area.

These are projects that I hope to roll out across the region as they are opportunities to develop the network of groups supporting people with dyslexia and their families, but, at the same time, maintaining their link with the local association.

Regional Development Work in the South East

Liz Tredget, Regional Development Officer

The local associations in the South East have been finding that more of the calls to their helplines are about adult dyslexics. Some associations are considering re-establishing adult support groups. We have made links with other organisations supporting other learning difficulties or disabilities and associations can now offer a wider range of support.

Links with the Connexions Service, Parent Partnership Networks (PPNs), Learning and Skills Councils (LSCs) and the South East Museum, Library and Archive Council (SEMLAC) are being formed. One local association has been involved in the development of a new library service and it is hoped to use this as a model for other authorities.

Project Work – Liverpool

Carmel Arnold, BDA Project Worker

"Dyslexia . . . It's not just about school".

This is the message that young dyslexic people want the Liverpool Dyslexia Project to give to service providers in the city. The project, funded by Liverpool Children's Fund, focuses on the fact that dyslexia affects the individual beyond the confines of the school building and school hours.

The project is working closely with a number of key agencies in the city, such as:

- The Connexions Service
- The Health Service
- Merseyside Youth Association
- The Play Service
- Supported Living – Children's Services and
- The Youth Offending Service

Each agency has identified a representative to sit on the steering group – a sure sign of their commitment to meet the needs of dyslexic young people. The LEA Special Needs section has a representative on the steering group too, ensuring the project complements the thriving dyslexia friendly schools programme in the city.

In its first year, the project has been able to offer dyslexia awareness raising to these larger key organisations as well as to a wide number of smaller agencies. Each organisation comes away with a knowledge of the differences associated with dyslexia – strengths and difficulties – and has an opportunity to consider how they might make themselves more dyslexia friendly. Some organisations have then chosen to work on a deeper level with the project to bring about real change. The Connexions Service, for instance, have requested training on screening processes and how to formulate action plans that better meet the needs of their dyslexic clients.

The project is working with the wider community too to raise awareness, having a presence at community events and, together with the local association, establishing two monthly drop-in sessions.

A key theme for the project is multi-agency working so that dyslexic children in the city are well supported wherever they are and whatever they are doing.

Project Work – Bradford, Manchester and West Yorkshire

Helen Boden, Former BDA Project Worker

Over the last twelve months my three project areas continued to develop and bring to light information that strengthens our resolve and demonstrates the need to develop a dyslexia friendly society.

The Bradford project, working with Bradford Youth Offending Team, has provided valuable information that illustrates the high incidence of dyslexia amongst young offenders. It also demonstrates the need to develop appropriate programmes of support and intervention, both within the youth justice system itself and within programmes that relate to education, training or employment. This project has also provided the opportunity to pilot support programmes and develop further research within this area.

The Manchester Project, working with JobCentre Plus, has also illustrated the need for accessible screening so that individuals can be signposted to appropriate opportunities to develop skills and achieve sustainable employment.

The New Dyslexia Visions Project in West Yorkshire is a groundbreaking innovation. For the first time the Learning and Skills Council (West Yorks) has provided a significant amount of money to examine the issue of dyslexia within the post-16 sector. The project encompasses areas from awareness training, screening, assessing and providing transitional support for school leavers through to basic skills, vocational support and support in employment, with a target of providing services to well over 1,000 beneficiaries. It has also provided the opportunity for the BDA and the Dyslexia Institute to pool resources and skills by working together to provide a comprehensive service within the region for individuals who are dyslexic.

BDA Information, Contacts and Publications

BDA website

Access the BDA website at www.bda-dyslexia.org.uk for all the contact details for:

- local dyslexia associations;
- supporting corporate members;
- BDA accredited courses.

You can also get contact details from our helpline – tel 0118 966 8271 or email info@dyslexiahelp-bda.demon.co.uk.

The website also contains a whole range of information on all aspects of dyslexia. Find out information on:

- where to obtain help;
- the latest BDA campaigns; and
- events being organised both nationally and at local level.

You can also alter the font and colour of the site and use Browsealoud which will read the text for you.

BDA Publications

In conjunction with R-E-M, you can access our publications catalogue or buy products online.
Go to www.bda-dyslexia.org.uk/main/shop.
Alternatively you can contact R-E-M direct as follows:

Tel: 01458 254 700
Fax: 01458 254 701

Address: BDA Publications
R-E-M
Great Western House
Langport
Somerset
TA10 9YU

Visit the BDA website: **www.bda-dyslexia.org.uk**

Dyslexia Contact

Access the word, access the world

Have you ever wondered how you can find out more about dyslexia?

Take a look at *Dyslexia Contact* – the official magazine of the British Dyslexia Association. Published 3 times a year, *Dyslexia Contact* is available to members and supporters of the organisation.

Dyslexia Contact covers a whole range of subjects and issues relating to dyslexia

- find out about the **latest developments** in the dyslexia world
- get **tips and hints** on living with dyslexia
- read about **inspirational** dyslexic people, such as Lee Ryan, former singer with the band Blue and Sir Jackie Stewart, motor racing legend
- get information on **services available** and how to access them
- wonder what kind of **computer software** is around
- find out about the **latest happenings** and campaigns in the BDA
- access **local support** and **local associations**
- **book reviews**

Dyslexia Contact is a lively, visual publication written in a dyslexia-friendly style that aims to provide impartial, practical information and advice for getting the best out of dyslexia. It is suitable for all with an interest in dyslexia including dyslexic people, parents, educators and related practitioners, institutions and corporate organisations.

For further details on how to receive *Dyslexia Contact* magazine please take a look at our website www.bda-dyslexia.org.uk or contact the Supporters' Mailing List Administrator at the BDA office on 0118 966 2677

Local Associations

Hilary Doody, Chair, Local Associations Board

The first contact with the BDA for some people is through a local association. There are nearly 100 affiliated associations in England, Wales and Northern Ireland.

What do they offer?

Associations are all different in the way they work. The activities and services that they provide will vary from one to another, but their aim is to provide support to their members and people in their local community. The range of services include:

- running a local helpline;
- organising meetings, workshops or conferences;
- publishing a newsletter;
- liaison with the local education authority and other agencies;
- Befrienders who support families in their efforts to obtain appropriate educational provision;
- circulation of Dyslexia Contact magazine;
- provision of dyslexia literature and materials for sale or for borrowing; and
- Computer Co-ordinators who provide support and information on IT issues.

One association is run by dyslexic adults specifically for dyslexic adults. In many parts of the country associations may have a separate adult group or adult Helpline.

One of the most important services that they offer is providing opportunities for people to talk to each other. Every association has people with a wealth of knowledge and experience. Sharing this knowledge and strategies to cope, as an individual or as a parent or teacher, can be invaluable. It helps to know that you are not alone, and that other people have had similar experiences. A parent commented to me recently:

> *"What you do is brilliant. I phoned your helpline several times and you saved my life. I can remember the pain of how it felt to have the diagnosis and the labels. You were the only people who understood."*

Several years later her son has a good understanding of how he learns differently and has a route to his chosen career in mind.

Mutual support can be given in many different ways; for example teachers and other professionals can learn from parents and dyslexic adults; adults may be a role model for children; children benefit from meeting other children with dyslexia; and parents can support each other.

How are they run?

Local Associations are all independent charities but they are affiliated to the BDA. Most are run by volunteers, often from their own homes, although some may have paid staff and offices. Volunteers include dyslexic adults, parents and teachers. Most associations charge their members a subscription and the amount varies from one association to another. They all have a management committee responsible for running the association.

How do you get the best from your local association?

It depends on what you need from the association. Many people get in touch when they have a specific problem, and they may contact the Helpline on several occasions over a period of time. Others come to meetings or talks of particular interest to themselves.

One of the best ways to learn more is to get involved. That might just mean joining the association, supporting it by attending events or by offering to help. There are so many different aspects to dyslexia and it takes time to learn and understand about it. The issues change from childhood to adolescence and in adult life. Whatever stage you are at, it is useful to know that you can share your concerns or your successes with other people and that you have a network of support around you.

The more people who are actively involved, the more your association can do to help you and other people locally.

How do local associations fit into BDA?

Associations are a vital part of the BDA, supporting the vision of the BDA and working in their own area to further the campaign aims of the BDA. With their invaluable and extensive local knowledge, local associations can do a lot at a local level to work to change systems and improve services for dyslexic people. In doing so they enhance the impact that the BDA makes on improving the lives of dyslexic people.

Local associations also have two Council Members who can attend and vote at national meetings and who elect a regional representative. In this way the views of dyslexic people and their families are heard at a national level and represented on the Management Board of the BDA. The BDA, in turn, offers a variety of support services to assist local associations in their extensive and ground-breaking role.

Where are they?

An up to date contact list can be found on the BDA website or the national helpline can provide information about your nearest association. If there is not one in your area, and you would be interested in getting a new group started, contact the Membership team at BDA for information.

BDA Web: www.bda-dyslexia.org.uk/main/membership
Tel (Helpline): 0118 966 8271
Tel (Membership): 0118 966 2677

Supporting Corporate Members

Louise Green, Chair of the Supporting Corporate Members' Committee

Companies and organisations that wish to support the BDA are encouraged to join as Supporting Corporate Members (SCMs). They are expected to:

- support the BDA vision;
- actively contribute professional expertise to BDA initiatives and campaign areas;
- agree to share information about their professional activities with other SCMs; and
- agree to abide by the membership code of conduct (see below).

There also are several conditions of membership and all SCMs must agree to abide by them.

Supporting Corporate Membership

Supporting Corporate Membership continues to grow and there are now around 140 organisations in the membership compared to 129 last year. These SCMs are divided into five main groups and, at the time of writing, there are:

- 17 specialist schools;
- 40 mainstream schools;
- 27 further education and higher education institutions;

- 28 teaching, teacher training and assessment centres; and
- 26 supplier organisations.

Representatives from each of these groups are voted on to the Supporting Corporate Members' Committee for a three year term. The number of members from each group is decided by proportional representation and all committee seats are rotated regularly to give a fair chance for all members to have a voice on the committee.

Supporting Corporate Members' Committee

The committee currently consists of members from:

- 2 specialist schools;
- 4 mainstream schools;
- 1 further education and higher education institutions;
- 3 teaching, teacher training and assessment centres; and
- 2 supplier organisations.

The committee meets three times a year. This year Rosie Wood completed her term of office as Chair and David Fulton completed his term as Vice Chair. I took over as Chair in February 2004 and Ros McCarthy, of Ellesmere College, became Vice Chair.

The Chair also holds a seat as a co-opted Trustee on the BDA Management Board.

Membership Criteria

The SCM conditions of membership were revised this year. SCM now are asked to abide by the following Code of Conduct:

- Supporting Corporate Members of the BDA must not make any claims to cure dyslexia.

- Supporting Corporate Members must not make claims for the success of their remediation or intervention unless these are supported by substantial independent research or evaluation.
- Supporting Corporate Members must not imply in any way that their BDA membership is a mark of approval, endorsement or quality assurance.
- Supporting Corporate Members must not abuse their membership privileges.

Activities

The SCM Committee aims to raise awareness of areas of concern for SCM members as well as to act on their behalf when appropriate. In the past year the SCMs Committee has been in touch with various organisations about:

- special examination arrangements;
- educational psychologist reports for adults;
- dyslexia friendly LEAs; and
- standards for assessing in further and higher education.

The Future

Since, by virtue of its role, responsibilities and position, the BDA aspires to be the voice of dyslexia, it needs to be seen to be representing the vast majority of dyslexic people. The support of all organisations dealing with dyslexia in any way whatsoever, therefore, is vital. The more SCMs that sign up to the BDA's vision and the SCM Code of Conduct, the stronger will be the BDA's position to help achieve the greatly desired dyslexia friendly society.

The BDA Accreditation Board

Professor Bob Burden, Chairman, Accreditation Board

One of the most important educational functions performed by the BDA is the monitoring and evaluation of training courses for teachers and learning support assistants working at every level with dyslexic students. In order to qualify for the right to offer its students the award of Associate Membership of the BDA (AMBDA), Approved Teacher Status (ATS), or Accredited Learning Support Assistant (ALSA), a training course is required to meet a number of stringent criteria relating to both the academic and professional aspects of training. AMBDA is the higher level qualification which requires a significantly greater degree of training and practice. There are also associated qualifications for those working in further and higher education.

The full criteria for all qualifications can be found on the BDA website at www.bda-dyslexia.org.uk/main/accreditation.

These qualifications have come to be seen as probably the strongest independent indicators of the quality of training for a teacher of children and adults with dyslexia that are currently available in this country. For this reason the BDA has always set the most stringent conditions for granting its awards and they are almost impossible to obtain without the prerequisite training.

The Accreditation Board in its current form was convened in 1994. Each of its Chairs have been Professors of Education at well established universities. They are independent and not involved with running dyslexia training courses. The Board consists of 16 members, many of whom represent the most significant training bodies for teachers and tutors of dyslexic students. Other members have been co-opted in order to provide extra specialist expertise. The current Vice-Chair is the BDA's Education Director, Professor Susan Tresman. Each member of the Board acts in a voluntary capacity.

The Board meets 3 times per year in London. The primary purpose of these meetings is to ratify personal applications for one of the awards and to provide ongoing accreditation for training courses. Currently we accredit 31 training courses for teachers and/or tutors and 10 training courses for learning support assistants. All courses are accredited for a period of 4 years, after which time it is necessary for them to apply for reaccreditation. Each course is given a liaison team consisting of two members of the Board. They make contact with the course directors, scrutinise available documentation and make visits where necessary. They then feed back their observation to the Board who make an informed decision.

Over the years this process has been found to work very well to the satisfaction of the vast majority of those involved. Even when a decision has not necessarily pleased an applicant or applying body, the scrupulous fairness of the Board in applying set criteria without fear or favour has almost always meant that decisions have been accepted as reasonable and unbiased.

The nature of the tasks undertaken by the Board over the past ten years has expanded markedly. The continuing professional development of teachers has come to be seen as a priority in view of the advances in knowledge and skills. This is quickly becoming a key area for the Board's consideration both in providing extra courses for AMBDA and ATS trained teachers and in insisting upon the need for individuals to update their qualifications. There has been a considerable extension of training into FE and HE institutions and mainstream schools with the drive towards the nationwide establishment of dyslexia friendly schools, colleges and universities. The influence of the Board on public examination arrangements for dyslexic students also continues to grow.

Accreditation Board meetings cover an enormous amount of work in a relatively brief amount of time. One of its most striking features is the way in which the representatives of what might otherwise be seen as rival bodies work harmoniously together as a team. It has been my privilege and pleasure to work with them.

The BDA Computer Committee

Victoria Crivelli, Chair, Computer Committee

The BDA Computer Commitee (BDACC) has been established for over 20 years. It was one of the first groups to recognise and explore the enormous potential of computer software to help children with dyslexia to learn to read and write and recognise that ICT had a place in education, in the workplace and at home.

The members of this forum in the early years were pioneers in ICT, demonstrating its use as a tool for learning and supporting literacy skills. They recognised its value for communicating and recording information, and promoting access to information on the internet. Software houses took note of their requests for dyslexia friendly programs with speech support and helpful screens.

Members were asked to speak at international conferences and exhibitions such as the BETT exhibition at Olympia in London. Many booklets were created to help and advise those who needed up to date information. These booklets were groundbreaking at that time. Jean Hutchins, a past chair of the committee, was particularly instrumental in setting the standard and establishing this role.

Today BDACC continues to be an established body that is recognised nationally and can help, advise and, in many cases, develop and support new initiatives in the use of ICT to help individuals with dyslexia.

For example key members have been instrumental in developing software for the assessment of dyslexia from early years through to adults. Similarly other members have been able to work closely with and influence software producers, web page writers and manufacturers of hardware and other ICT tools.

Today the use of ICT is widely recognised at work, home and in education. It continues to be a key tool to support not only those with dyslexia but many adults and children with other learning and access needs.

BDACC continues to develop and extend the role and good practice established by the original membership. We continue to support and advise BDA, local groups and individuals through talks, seminars, meetings, telephone support, articles in publications such as Dyslexia Contact, the BDA magazine, booklets, web page information, responding and partaking in BDA Forum, being available (and approachable) for advice at exhibitions and reviewing new software. We continue to work with software writers and producers, striving to improve products to meet the needs of individuals.

We help with the software and BDA publications leaflet published by REM. We advise schools and colleges, parents and teachers, as well as employers. We work with professionals, both nationally and internationally, evaluating and sharing good practice.

Current members represent a wide range of skills and expertise and many are working full time in a diversity of professions. These include:

- specialist teachers;
- ICT consultants;
- educational psychologists;
- university lecturers; and
- LDA members and Befrienders.

Many members are recognised nationally for their work and expertise. All BDACC members are volunteers and give their time freely, as do so many other volunteers for local and national dyslexia associations. Some members have specific interests or responsibilities.

We meet three times a year to plan seminars, produce information and help initiate and support projects. The meetings also provide opportunities for members to share information, demonstrate software and hardware and discuss the latest developments. ICT is moving so much faster these days compared with the early years, so this communication is vital. In between meetings we communicate regularly by email to continue our support and carry out our work individually and collectively. More recently we have tried to develop ways of offering advice to local areas for exhibitions, talks and ICT clinics. We are currently trying to develop ways of keeping information as up to date as possible and avoid too many paper based booklets that can date so quickly.

Four BDACC members will be presenting seminars at the BETT international exhibition in January 2005. They and other members will also be available on the BDA stand to offer advice to visitors during that time.

Current members include:

- Victoria Crivelli (Chair)
- EA Draffan
- Di Hillage
- Jeff Hughes
- Anita Keates
- Ian Litterick
- Dr Chris Singleton
- Judith Stansfield
- Barry Whiting (chair elect)

The BDA Music Committee

John Westcombe, Chair, Music Committee

This group of widely experienced people has a history of over 20 years. It began life as an idea of Pam Smith, who worked for the Disabled Living Foundation. Daphne Kennard was also involved and soon the original 12 page BDA booklet on Music and Dyslexia appeared. The names of Violet Brand, Margaret Hubicki, Tim Miles and Caroline Beaumont – still in the dyslexia public eye – have been associated with, or members of, the committee from the start. The BDA generously took over the funding of meetings etc from the Disabled Living Foundation.

Booklets were revised, but the committee soon realised that a major undertaking – indeed a substantial book – was necessary to boost its main aim of raising awareness of how dyslexia affects music learning and playing. Whurr was chosen as publisher and committee members contributed chapters, together with those from a further group, who brought inspiration and encouragement from their own angles. (*Music and Dyslexia*, Miles and Westcombe (eds), 2001). That and committee member Sheila Oglethorpe's own book (*Instrumental Music for Dyslexics*), also published by Whurr have been very well received.

The committee has a wide range of interests, with academics, authors, teachers in conservatoire schools and private practice, professional players and singers, from England, Scotland and Ireland. (Tim Miles, Violet Brand and

Margaret Hubicki have been honoured by the Queen.) It is consulted on various matters, recently by senior members of the Associated Board of the Royal Schools of Music, both about grade examinations, and through tutoring on their professional development work with teachers across the country.

Individually, members have spoken at high level conferences of LEAs and professional associations and sought to persuade teacher training institutions to include more guidance about dyslexia and music. As a group, the members bring wide ranging experiences to lively debates, for example, about approaches to sight reading!

On a month by month basis, the committee responds to correspondence, latterly from USA and Germany. It also keeps abreast of research, particularly in the neuroscience area, and seeks information from teachers experienced in dyslexia and music who might wish to extend their work. Local associations might be able to help us in this.

A list of committee names and brief biographies appeared in *Dyslexia Contact* in May 2004 (Vol. 23, No. 2) and a two-page article on Anne Marie Sand, professional singer appeared in Vol. 23, No. 1 published in January 2004.

Review of the 6th BDA International Conference

Angela Fawcett, Conference Chair, and Lindsay Peer, Conference Consultant

The benefits of an international conference cannot be overestimated, both in terms of strengthening ties between theory and practice and bringing together the whole of the dyslexia ecosystem in one venue. The conference took place in March 2004 at the University of Warwick. It attracted speakers and delegates from 35 countries, making it a truly international event. The atmosphere throughout was electric!

In this article we will present some of the highlights of the conference. Angela will be focusing on theory and Lindsay on policy and practice. We had over 300 speakers and there is unfortunately no way that we can mention them all and their topics, but we will attempt to give you a highlight of just a few. It is our hope that together we can give you some flavour of the 2004 conference.

The conference started with an introduction from Lindsay followed by some beautiful singing from the girls of the Coventry Cathedral Choir. This was followed by a stirring plea for recognition of the positive aspects of dyslexia from our opening speaker, Tom West, author of *In the Mind's Eye*.

Building on this theme, Daniel Tresman talked about some of the struggles and the achievements he was most proud of as a young dyslexic student. Daniel is the 17 year old son of Professor Susan Tresman, the Education Director at the BDA.

In Angela's keynote, which followed, she showed that all the theories of dyslexia can be seen as compatible. We can build on our greater understanding of dyslexia to address more of the problems arising for children and young people with dyslexia.

A symposium on the causal theories of dyslexia proposed by Padraic Monaghan at the University of Warwick took up the themes raised by Angela's keynote on the first afternoon. The keynote speaker, Guinevere Eden gave an accessible talk on theory into practice. She illustrated her talk with information on the fMRI techniques she runs with young children at the University of Georgetown, Washington. The day finished with dancing to a jazz band, and a chance to escape from the stress of the day.

The second day started with an inspired keynote from Professor Aryan van der Leij, on working with dyslexia in an inflexible system. Two further keynotes took place, including Dr John Rack outlining the findings of the Spellit Project, which used parents in delivering a battery of support for spelling. The final keynote of the day, by Professor Ginger Berninger outlined the effectiveness of remedial techniques that actually altered the way that the brain works, in children with dyslexia, after an intensive 3 week intervention.

In addition to the seven parallel sessions of symposia and papers, a series of four parallel sessions of workshops were presented daily, to allow delegates some hands on experience in small groups. A strong poster session was also presented in the afternoon. In the evening the Mayor's

Reception gave us all the opportunity to get together, share a glass of wine, and announce the winners of the Psychological Corporation's prize for outstanding postgraduate research in dyslexia. This year it went to Tomi Guttorm for his work on speech recognition in infants with a family history of dyslexia. This was followed by a series of informal seminars, including a meeting to discuss benchmarking of complementary interventions.

The third day started with a keynote by Dr Lindsay Peer CBE on policy changes in the UK. This was followed by the themed programme of symposia, papers and workshops. The day culminated with a strong poster session. In the evening there was a formal dinner with Sir Steve Redgrave CBE as our guest speaker. As a dyslexic himself, Sir Steve was able to contribute to our understanding of dyslexia, sharing with us that he had only ever read 4 books, and that 2 of these he had written himself with the help of his wife.

The final day started with a moving keynote from Dr Reid Lyon, who is in charge of the $60 million annual budget for US research. This is a very different situation from that found in the UK where relatively little is given to research. It culminated with the final keynote from Professor Rod Nicolson, assessing the progress made in addressing the needs of the ecosystem since the 2001 conference.

The conference ended with a series of round tables where both speakers and delegates were able to voice their opinions on changes they consider necessary for the future.

There have been excellent working relationships over many years with government bodies in the UK and much progress has been made in terms of policy and practice. It should be noted that the DfES gave this conference every support, guidance and encouragement, for which we are all very grateful.

For three out of the four days of the conference there was an excellent exhibition organised by Educational Events Limited.

There are many materials still available to purchase from the conference. These are:

- A CD ROM, which includes the majority of the speakers' talks and their PowerPoint presentations. This costs £29.38.
- A textbook entitled "Dyslexia in Context: Research, Policy and Practice", edited by Gavin Reid and Angela Fawcett, and published by Whurr. It includes chapters written by selected presenters. This costs £30.00 plus postage and handling costs.
- A DfES sponsored book entitled "Dyslexia: Perspectives for Classroom Practitioners". A limited number of copies are still available at a cost of £5.00.
- Two special editions of the BDA's journal 'Dyslexia' highlighted the main themes of the conference. These were edited by Joel Talcott.

For further details on any of the above resources, please contact the BDA.

The conference had renewed many old friendships, and forged new ones. We hope that we have been able to capture some the excitement and tension of an international conference and that you will be inspired to join the BDA at the next International Conference, whether as speaker or delegate!

MOON HALL SCHOOL

Moon Hall School, Feldemore, Holmbury St. Mary, Dorking, Surrey RH5 6LQ
Telephone: 01306 731464 Fax: 01306 731504
e-mail:enquiries@moonhall.surrey.sch.uk web address: www.moonhall.surrey.sch.uk
Head Teacher: Mrs J. Lovett, Cert. Ed., AMBDA Founded: 1985 by Mrs B.E. Baker

Status: Independent DfES registered 936/6551
CReSTeD accredited – Category SP

Age range: 7–11 full time
7–13 part time
Number of Teaching Staff: 16
Type: Mixed

Number at Moon Hall:
51 full time
62 part-time
Total Number on site: 240
Weekly Boarding and Day.

Children with Specific Learning Difficulties/Dyslexia benefit from the unique arrangement of a specialist school within a main-stream preparatory school.

Specialist facilities: Full time specialist classes offer a complete curriculum for children aged 7–10, whilst for those over 10, teaching is shared with the Prep. School. Children may attend Moon Hall for specialist tuition in English and Mathematics at all levels. All children benefit from a wide variety of available resources.

General Environment: Moon Hall is in an attractive, homely building in the grounds of Belmont Preparatory School. It shares the facilities of Belmont, including Gym, Dining Room, Library, D&T and I.C.T. facilities, Science Lab, Playing Fields and outdoor Swimming Pool. Belmont School itself is based in an historic Victorian mansion set in 60 acres of wooded grounds. It is mid-way between Dorking and Guildford.

Aims and Philosophy: At Moon Hall we aim to offer sympathetic help to children whose dyslexia affects their ability to learn in a normal classroom. We have helped many highly intelligent dyslexic children to realise their true potential.

Our priority is to restore confidence and to develop a positive attitude to learning. We do this by providing a happy, family atmosphere with support and understanding for each child. However, the demands of any one child are realistically balanced against the needs of the group as a whole.

Children are carefully assessed and given a structured programme appropriate to their needs. The Phono-Graphix reading programme is in use with most of our pupils. This means that they achieve early success on which we can build. We also give them new skills and tools to overcome their difficulties and to build their self esteem. All are taught to touch-type from the age of 7. All benefit from a wide range of specialist reading and spelling computer software. We seek to develop each child's strengths as well as working to overcome their difficulties. Study Skills (including learning techniques, memory strategies, organisation skills etc.) are an important part of our curriculum. Work is based upon the National Curriculum and Common Entrance Examination where appropriate. Our eventual aim is to return any child who is able, to a mainstream class – usually Belmont – with ongoing support.

Home/School Links: Moon Hall School has close links with all parents. Regular written reports are issued – including syllabus reports. There are Parents' Evenings and talks about our work. A thriving and well-supported PTA exists and this organises social functions and fund raising events. Boarding at Belmont is on a weekly basis and children are therefore free for a full family weekend from Fridays at 4.30 p.m.

Staff qualifications: All staff are fully qualified in their own field and each member of the English Staff has a Diploma in the Assessment and Teaching of Children with Specific Learning Difficulties/Dyslexia. Staff regularly attend National Conferences etc. and we are involved in several areas of important research. All staff now have an additional Phono-Graphix qualification.

Looking forward to the 3rd International Multilingual and Dyslexia Conference

Multilingual and Cross-Cultural Perspectives on Dyslexia

The international conferences on multilingualism and dyslexia were born from a highly successful collaboration between BDA, the European Dyslexia Association (EDA) and the International Dyslexia Association (IDA). The first conference was held in Manchester, UK in 1999 and the second in Washington DC, USA in 2002.

The 3rd International Multilingual and Dyslexia Conference takes place from 14–16 July 2005 in Limassol, Cyprus, and is being co-ordinated mainly by EDA and the Cyprus Dyslexia Association. It is chaired by H. Alan Sayles, EDA President, and Lindsay Peer, international dyslexia consultant.

Purpose

The purpose of this conference is to increase our understanding on Multilingual and Cross-Cultural Perspectives of Dyslexia. The target audience includes:

- classroom and special education teachers;

- dyslexia and specific learning disability specialists;
- cross-linguistic and cross-cultural researchers;
- psychologists;
- medical and legal professionals;
- speech and language therapists;
- English as a Second Language and foreign language teachers; and
- clinical and school administrators.

It is anticipated that this will be one of the largest International Dyslexia Conferences held so far with approximately 500 participants from Europe, USA, Israel and Cyprus.

Speakers

Five international keynote speakers will share their knowledge and expertise giving a chance for delegates to gain more insight to the world of multilingualism and dyslexia. They are:

- Dr Nata Goulandris, University College, London, UK
- Dr Esther Geva, University of Toronto, Ontario, Canada.
- Dr Lindsay Peer, International Dyslexia Consultant
- Dr R. Malatesha Joshi, Texas A & M University
- Dr George Th. Pavlidis, University of Macedonia

In the symposia and workshops participants will be able to hear some of the foremost educators and researchers in the field. There will also be opportunities for everyone attending the conference to share and exchange information and ideas.

Symposia Themes

- Multilingualism and Dyslexia
- Policy on Dyslexia
- Identification and Assessment
- Foreign Language Teaching and Dyslexia
- Phonological Skills
- Dyslexia and the Brain
- Teaching and Learning for Multilingual Dyslexic Learners
- Information Technology

The symposia themes are subject to change according to the seminar proposals. Other themes may also be considered.

Call for Papers

The Call for Papers is now available. 300 word proposals may be submitted for symposia (3–4 presenters with facilitators), or for individual sessions. Some of these may be grouped as a series addressing specific themes. Proposals for workshops and posters are particularly invited.

Speakers who are accepted for presentation will have their registration fees waived for the day(s) they are scheduled to present. Accepted speakers are expected to pay for their own transport, accommodation, meals and special events. Guidelines for submitting an abstract are available on the conference website at www.3rd-dyslexia-international.org.

The deadline for submission is 15 February 2005 and submissions should be sent to Alan Sayles at asayles@iolfree.ie.

Further Information

The special conference website is now live at www.3rd-dyslexia-international.org. It contains details of the Call for Papers, the preliminary programme and how to apply. For further information please contact:

Kalia Kitsis
Conference Coordinator
Highway Communications
Kalia.k@highwaycommunications.com
Website: www.HIGHWAYCOMMUNICATIONS.COM
Tel: +357 22 340909 Fax: +357 22 340934

OTHER DYSLEXIA ORGANISATIONS:

Bangor Dyslexia Unit

Liz Du Pré, Student Service, Bangor Dyslexia Unit

If there are themes that characterise the work of the Dyslexia Unit at Bangor they are to a large part, concerned with continuity and change. In the various aspects of the Unit's work, its teaching, student and assessment services, we are fortunate to be able to build on and develop a steady tradition of good practice. From the Unit's earliest days, this practice has not only been informed by the findings of research. It has also been underpinned by a philosophy: we support individuals – children, students and adults – from whom we, in turn, have much to learn.

Continuity

The roots of the Unit's approach lie in the work of Tim Miles. Now an Emeritus Professor, Tim continues to provide inspiration and sound sense. The last year has seen the publication of new editions of *Dyslexia and Stress* and of *Dyslexia and Mathematics*. Tim's forty years of work was honoured in 2003, when he was awarded an OBE in recognition of his contributions to the field of dyslexia.

Change

The Dyslexia Unit is part of the School of Psychology at the University of Wales, Bangor (UWB). This year has seen its position strengthened with the proposal to link the Unit with the Language and Learning Group in the School. The advantages of this will be two-way: the Unit can contribute practical expertise, and benefit from the ongoing research and debate around dyslexia-related language and learning issues.

Teaching

The Unit's teaching service has a longstanding partnership with local LEAs. It organises a team of around 60 part time specialist teachers who provide tuition in primary and secondary schools. Also arranged for independent schools, or for private pupils, teaching may be in English or Welsh – or both, depending on individuals' needs.

The demand continues for support for literacy development but a growing number of pupils are referred for support with maths. At the secondary level, teachers are also involved in developing study skills. and with curriculum support. The flexible framework for our teaching is described in *The Bangor Dyslexia Teaching System* by Elaine Miles and *Tackling Dyslexia* by Ann Cooke. Unit teachers have also developed widely used Welsh resource materials: *O Gam I Gam* by Elisabeth Griffiths and *Camu 'Mlaen* by Nêst Tudor Efans and Helen Vaughan Williams.

The Unit supports its teachers with up-to-date resources (photocopiable materials, books, games, software, including Bangor's own Xavier software, maths equipment, and test materials). Teachers meet regularly for in-service training, and for workshops on specific topics. Valuing working relationships with parents, as well as with schools, we run workshops and produce support booklets for parents, and provide staff awareness and training sessions in schools.

Student Service

Over 360 dyslexic UWB students (undergraduate and postgraduate) are registered with the Unit's Student Service. Many come for individual support with managing course work or to develop study skills. Others like to 'check in' and have a chat about how things are going. Students value this dedicated dyslexia support centre on their doorstep and our tutors (full and part time) and administrative staff are always welcoming, ready to listen or offer advice on issues ranging from time management, to problems with computers. A regular newsletter keeps all students in touch, and a student support group meets weekly in the Unit: an opportunity for students to share and extend their strategies for study and survival at university.

Within the university the Unit liaises on students' behalf with admissions, academic, library and exam office staff. The extending of the Disability Discrimination Act to higher education has brought closer co-operation with UWB's central Student Services, to enhance the university's inclusive approach to admitting, teaching and assessing dyslexic students; again the Unit has become more fully integrated into the wider university structure, providing advice, and awareness sessions for staff and students, and drawing up Personal Learning Support Plans between students and their departments.

Often referred by departments, students come for assessment for dyslexia: we offer pre-assessment screenings, and counselling advice after the psychologists' assessments. With the UWB Access Centre, we assist students applying for the Disabled Students' Allowance and carry out study needs assessments for this.

We have recently revised two popular booklets, available from the Unit: *Applying to University for Dyslexic Students* and *Dyslexic Students at University: a Guide for Staff*.

Assessments

Our three visiting Educational Psychologists assess children and adults, as well as students from UWB and other colleges in the region. We also offer specialist teacher assessments and are developing an assessment for dyscalculia. The Unit has recently appointed a full time psychologist to meet the growing demand.

Courses

Two part-time courses (BDA accredited) are available for teachers wishing to specialise in dyslexia: the one-year Course of Further Professional Studies, and three modules towards an MEd/Diploma in Education. Lectures take place over five weekends and both courses involve teaching practice.

Advice and Information

For advice and information about our services, or any of the publications mentioned in this article, contact:

The Dyslexia Unit
University of Wales, Bangor,
Gwynedd, LL57 2DG
Tel: 01248 382203/Fax: 01248 382614
Email: dyslex-admin@bangor.ac.uk
Website: www.dyslexia.bangor.ac.uk

Dyslexia Institute

Shirley Cramer, Chief Executive

Founded in 1972, The Dyslexia Institute (DI) is the largest independent provider of assessment and tuition for dyslexic people in the UK, having a nationwide network of 27 main centres and 140 smaller teaching units. In addition, the Institute runs teacher training courses, develops specialist teaching materials and conducts research.

DI National Training and Resource Centre

The DI's Head Office and National Training and Resource Centre are located at Park House, Egham, Surrey, on the edge of Windsor Great Park and within easy reach of the M25.

Assessment Services

Last year the DI assessed over 7,500 children and adults. DI assessment is carried out by 70 consulting psychologists who work under the supervision of our staff psychologists and receive regular updating on the latest materials and techniques to ensure a high standard of service throughout the UK.

In addition to full psychological assessments carried out by psychologists, we also offer educational assessments by specially trained teachers, assessments for special arrangements for examinations, and a range of group screenings for schools and other bodies. Assessments are carried out in all main DI centres.

Specialist Teaching

The DI currently employs 250 specialist teachers all of whom have postgraduate SpLD qualifications. We operate a continuous professional development programme to ensure that teachers benefit from the most up-to-date research and practice.

Some 3,000 students, both children and adults, are taught each year in our centres and smaller units, 70% of which are based in schools. All the main centres offer individual and small group teaching and many now work very closely with LEAs and other agencies to provide specialist tuition and to raise awareness of dyslexia in mainstream schools.

The majority of DI students are school-aged children who are struggling in school and need specialist help. All work on individual programmes designed to meet their specific needs. Our teaching uses two widely acclaimed literacy programmes – the Dyslexia Institute Literacy Programme and Units of Sound Multimedia – both of which are continually improved and evaluated. The Dyslexia Institute Maths Programme is also very popular with teachers.

Working in Partnership

The DI is increasingly involved in partnership projects with other organisations including BDA. Many of these involve working with schools to improve support for children with literacy difficulties and at the same time raising awareness of dyslexia among the school community and enhancing the specialist expertise of staff. Other projects include those designed to promote adult literacy, to carry out specialist research and to produce specialist resources.

Support for Parents

The DI recently produced the Dyslexia Institute Young Readers' Support Pack for parents – its first resource directly targeting parents and carers – which resulted from an extensive three-year research programme. The resource, which is proving extremely popular, is designed for parents of young children just starting to read, and older children who need additional help. The DIY Readers' Support Pack for parents and other specialist resources are available from our Head Office or via the Resources Shop on our website at www.dyslexia-inst.org.uk.

Focusing on Adults

There are many undiagnosed adults in the UK and few services for them. Many are ill equipped for employment and desperately need to develop both their skills and their self-esteem. Continual failure has made this the most vulnerable group of dyslexic individuals.

The DI teaches over 400 adults who range from university students to those with very few literacy skills. Our multimedia Adult Literacy Programme, which is closely linked to the Government's Adult Core Curriculum, now forms the basis of our "Supporting Adults in Dyslexia and Literacy" course for tutors of dyslexic adults. A booklet, *Best Practice for Adults,* and leaflets, *Information for Employers, Studying with Dyslexia*, and *Do you think you may be dyslexic?* are all now available.

The DI continues to work with the Probation and Prison services to help dyslexic adults. The PALS (Positive Action through Learning Support) Project with Nottinghamshire Probation Service has continued to expand and is a Home Office pathfinder project to evaluate the outcomes of improving literacy amongst probation clients.

Specialist Teacher Training

The largest barrier to improved services for individuals with dyslexia is the shortage of specialist teachers. The DI Training Service continues to develop new courses to overcome this problem. We now offer a two-year Postgraduate Diploma and a one-year Postgraduate Certificate. Both are available in a number of locations and the Certificate course can also be followed by distance learning. These courses, which are validated by the University of York, are partly funded by the Teacher Training Agency.

Other courses run by our Training Department include those for teaching assistants, mainstream teachers and SENCOs, and tutors in Further Education and Basic Skills provision. Tailor-made INSET for schools, and workplace training for employers, are also available. Further details can be found in our Training Prospectus which is available on our website.

Research and Development

The DI is committed to constant evaluation of its own practices and to working with other researchers to improve its teaching. We completed the three year SPELLIT research project in 2002, which was the most significant evaluation of specialist teaching for younger children ever conducted in the UK. The project's findings endorsed the DI's teaching methods but have also inspired further research and development.

Resource Centre

The Resource Centre, which has open membership, holds a vast range of books and materials which are available for loan by members. Further details can be obtained from its website at www. dyslexiaresourcecentre.com or by calling 01784 222352.

The Dyslexia Institute Guild

The Dyslexia Institute Guild is the DI's professional body. Membership is available to any individual with an interest in dyslexia and includes teachers trained by the DI, other specialist teachers, psychologists, speech and language therapists, special needs teachers and mainstream classroom teachers. The Guild aims to keep members up to date on developments in the field. To achieve this it publishes a termly professional journal, *Dyslexia Review*, holds an Annual Symposium and provides regular newsletters reviewing the DI's activities.

DI Bursary Fund

The DI Bursary Fund is a separate charity, established in 1982, to fund lessons for those who are unable to meet the full cost of tuition. Currently some 250 students receive support.

For further details of DI Centres and services provided please contact our head office at:

The Dyslexia Institute
Park House
Wick Road
Egham
Surrey TW20 0HH
Tel: 01784 222 300 Fax: 01784 222 333
Email: *info@dyslexia-inst.org.uk*
Website: www.dyslexia-inst.org.uk

Helen Arkell Dyslexia Centre

Rosie Wood, Executive Director

What are we?

The Helen Arkell Dyslexia Centre (HADC) is the oldest dyslexia centre in the country. Our founder and life President, Helen Arkell, started the Centre in London in 1971 with just two colleagues. We are immensely proud that she was invited to Buckingham Palace in November 2003 as one of the Pioneers of the 20th Century. Helen actively supports all aspects of the Centre's work and we strive to keep alive her original intentions:

- to offer expert help to anyone with dyslexia, regardless of their ability to pay; and
- to maintain a friendly, warm and individual approach whilst giving rigorously professional support.

A registered charity, the Centre has a bursary fund to subsidise services for those who cannot afford the fees. Fund raising incorporates donations, events and support from trusts and companies; the Centre is indebted to the generosity of all its donors.

Who are we?

The Centre is a thriving body of experienced and expert staff, including specialist teachers, educational psychologists, speech and language therapists, tutors and occupational therapists – all supported by a tireless administration staff!

Where are we?

Deep in the heart of leafy Surrey near Farnham, down a bumpy lane, in the middle of fields and woods, in a welcoming and friendly building.

Why are we here?

The Centre exists to offer individualised learning solutions to those with specific learning difficulties (SpLD)/dyslexia. Each client is recognised as unique and support is tailored to maximise strengths and minimise weaknesses. HADC enables individuals with SpLD/dyslexia to become independent so that each can reach their full potential in education, employment and the community. This mission extends through all our activities and training.

What do we offer?

A dyslexia 'one stop shop' with a wide range of services to:

- support dyslexic people and their families; and
- offer training and support to professionals.

These services include:

- **Consultations and Assessments.** Often the first contact for a client is an initial consultation with a senior professional staff member, to discuss options. Assessments should be tailored to an individual's needs so we offer a wide variety with different professionals. Time is always allowed for full discussion and reports are user friendly and focus on positive ways to help the individual achieve potential. Recommendations are plentiful and practical.
- **Tuition and Courses for People with SpLD/dyslexia.** One to one (and small group) specialist tuition/therapy is given by experienced specialist teachers and therapists. Short courses are held at weekends and during holidays,

including a popular programme of summer schools. These courses focus on study skills, social interaction skills, and, for parents, 'how to help your own child'. A literacy course for young adults is run one evening a week in term time. Other ad hoc courses are arranged as needs arise. Speech and language therapy and occupational therapy are arranged where needed.

- **Professional Training.** Training courses are run each year for teachers and classroom assistants. These have nationally recognised qualifications by the OCR (Oxford, Cambridge and RSA Board). Most are at Frensham and some are off site. Recently we have added courses for Basic Skills tutors. Short courses run throughout the year to update professionals on topical subjects.
- **Conferences.** Each year an annual conference is held either in Cambridge or in South East England. These conferences attract an international audience.
- **INSET and Awareness Training.** Insets to schools, colleges and businesses are a growing area of activity. Senior professional staff travel throughout the UK to raise awareness and offer training, practical support and ideas in order to help professional colleagues provide a truly inclusive education and community.
- **Research.** As funds allow, the Centre carries out research. With its network of contacts, the Centre is especially well placed to conduct research into methodology. The most recent research, supported by the DfES, focused on discovering children's most effective methods for learning spelling.
- **Bookshop.** The Alexandra Rose Day Resources Library contains a specialist bookshop, stocking titles of interest to both professionals and parents as well as dyslexic adults. The resource catalogue is on the website.

Many of the Centre's services are available to organisations through partnership schemes. Currently we have a project with Feltham Young Offenders Institution, training their Learning Support Assistants and providing Insets for staff, and assessment and teaching for inmates. Following a successful partnership with the London Borough of Sutton, we have begun a similar scheme with Southwark; teachers from the borough are training at the Centre and further support is planned for schools in Southwark. A partnership scheme with the Royal Borough of Windsor and Maidenhead has successfully achieved a dyslexia intervention programme for Key Stages 1 and 2 and will work towards Key Stage 3 in 2005.

The Future?

Our Centre has grown and we have plans for further modest expansion. Refurbishment of our premises, additional space and an increase in staff are among this year's plans. With our supportive Trustee Board, we share a feeling of cheerful optimism and remain determined to offer the highest possible level of service to the dyslexic community.

Helen Arkell Dyslexia Centre
Frensham
Farnham
Surrey GU10 3BW
Tel: 01252 792400
Fax: 01252 795669
Email: enquiries@arkellcentre.org.uk
Web: www.arkellcentre.org.uk

Developments at the Hornsby International Dyslexia Centre

Tilly Mortimore, Distance Learning Course Director

The Hornsby International Dyslexia Centre has been a well known name in the training of teachers by distance learning for many years.

Our well known Hornsby Diploma Course has been revised to include the latest practical and theoretical developments to support dyslexic learners. It combines lectures by cutting edge academics and practitioners, with individual tutorial support in teaching practice. It provides a flexible range of approaches allowing students to follow their interests and develop programmes to meet the needs of dyslexic learners of all ages within all contexts. This can all be achieved without attendance, through the medium of distance learning. This has proved very attractive to students with other commitments or who live in distant places.

We have been particularly keen to encourage teachers and teaching assistants around the world to take up specialist training in dyslexia as there is increasing evidence of need in international schools wherever English is a major teaching language. We are therefore delighted by the developments in our distance learning programmes as we feel that the new course offers a flexible way for students, wherever they live, to develop a range of skills to meet their training needs

In the summer of 2003 we also set up in partnership with Kingston University to provide access to a Postgraduate Diploma in Professional Studies in Education in Specific Learning Difficulties/Dyslexia by distance learning. This can offer 120 CATS points – two thirds of a Masters degree. We have a growing number of students enrolling on this course and the feedback has been very enthusiastic. There is now a possibility that students may be able to complete the final third of their Masters with Kingston University.

We run an established and well regarded attendance course to train teaching assistants to work with dyslexic learners. This course is recognised by the BDA. We are now in the process of developing delivery of this training by distance learning. This will be fitted into the Government framework for training advanced teaching assistants.

From the Centre in Clapham, London, where you can purchase books and resources, we run a range of attendance courses and conferences and carry out assessments.

If you would like to hear more about what we offer, please log on to our new website at www.hornsby.co.uk. Alternatively email us at dyslexia@hornsby.co.uk or telephone 020 7223 1144.

Dyslexia Scotland

Dyslexia Scotland is the umbrella organisation for dyslexia branches and groups in Scotland. The headquarters is located in Stirling.

Dyslexia Scotland and its network of branches strive to raise awareness of the nature of dyslexia and how it can affect children, young people, and adults in all aspects of their daily lives. We provide a service which is unique in Scotland, giving advice, information, and support to dyslexic people, their families, teachers, employers and to other professionals who have an interest in dyslexia.

On behalf of dyslexic people in Scotland, we respond to consultation documents issued by the Scottish Executive and aim to influence the educational policy of both central and local government. Dyslexia Scotland representatives attend meetings of formal and informal bodies to ensure that the voice of dyslexic people in Scotland is heard.

We also work with many statutory bodies including Adult Literacy & Numeracy, the Scottish Prison Service and various employers. We have recently worked in partnership with Communities Scotland to deliver a handbook to every volunteer tutor in Scotland to assist in teaching dyslexic adults. This is a major initiative to raise awareness of dyslexia in the adult sector.

Dyslexia Scotland has resumed its roadshows to outlying areas of Scotland. These roadshows aim to target specific areas to raise awareness and to encourage the formation of

new branches. Resources, books and materials are taken to various venues for people to browse. Qualified, knowledgeable staff are on hand to provide advice, and workshop sessions are provided free of charge for anyone attending.

Last year the roadshow was organised to coincide with Dyslexia Awareness Week. It is hoped to run another roadshow during Dyslexia Awareness Week 2005.

Dyslexia Scotland has many services to offer including:

Dyslexia Helpline: A confidential telephone helpline service manned by experienced knowledgeable staff. The helpline is open Monday to Friday from 10.00 am until 4.00 pm. If a caller wishes to discuss individual circumstances with an independent person, Dyslexia Scotland has dyslexia advisers who can assist.

Membership: Anyone can become a member of Dyslexia Scotland for a nominal annual subscription. Members are kept up to date on advances in the world of dyslexia as well as on the activities of Dyslexia Scotland and its local branches. Dyslexia Scotland is a member of various organisations including:

- Scottish Council of Voluntary Organisation (SCVO);
- Volunteer Development Scotland (VDS); and
- Learning Link Scotland.

Dyslexia Scotland also has reciprocal membership with a number of voluntary organisations including:

- SKILL (Scotland);
- Hornsby International Dyslexia Centre; and
- British Dyslexia Association.

National Tutor List: This is an "information only" service and there is no financial arrangement between Dyslexia Scotland and the tutors on our list. Each tutor will have his or her own scale of charges. A tutor on our register is normally expected to hold a specialised qualification in the teaching of dyslexic people and preferably also to hold a teaching qualification.

Presentations: Dyslexia Scotland is experienced in presenting workshops, talks and seminars for all manner of situations. These can be arranged for professional and non-professional groups with in-service training designed to suit individual requirements. We also hold a national conference each year in September. This conference is attended by a wide cross section of people within the education field. Previous keynote speakers include Professor Usha Goswami,

Dr Angela Fawcett, Professor John Stein and many other eminent professionals.

Assessments: Dyslexia Scotland can arrange psychological assessments at its HQ in Stirling, and can provide details of other psychologists throughout Scotland.

What of the Future?

The increasing number of calls to the helpline suggests that there is a great deal of work to be done to ensure that dyslexic children receive the help necessary to enable them to achieve their full potential in the education system. By analysing the calls, and taking account of feedback from branches, Dyslexia Scotland knows that there is good practice in some local education authority areas. However, in other areas the level of provision is still poor but we will continue to encourage good practice wherever possible.

The helpline is receiving more and more calls from dyslexic adults seeking help. Dyslexia Scotland has formed an Adult Network made up of members and non-members from throughout Scotland. Regular seminars are held to harness their thoughts and ideas on how to progress support for this particular sector of the dyslexia community.

For further details contact:

Dyslexia Scotland
Stirling Business Centre
Wellgreen, Stirling, FK8 2DZ

Dyslexia Helpline Scotland: 01786 446650

European Dyslexia Association

H. Alan Sayles, President

The European Dyslexia Association (EDA) is a European-based, international umbrella organisation. We seek to provide an information network for parents and professional organisations whose main concern is the welfare of individuals with dyslexia. The EDA is a recognised charity, founded in Belgian law in 1987 by representatives of national dyslexia associations in Belgium, Denmark, France, Germany, Ireland, Netherlands, Norway and the United Kingdom.

The principal aims of the EDA are:

1 to assist and develop support for people with dyslexia in their educational, social and cultural integration into society;
2 to promote co-operation between parents, teachers and other professionals;
3 to publish news of its activities and to encourage research into cause(s), diagnosis, intervention and prevention; and
4 to carry out comparative studies and to co-operate world-wide with other organisations with similar aims.

The EDA welcomes contact with other interested organisations that would like be considered for membership. The work of the EDA is led by a Board of Directors which is elected at a General Assembly of the members held every two years. The board meets three times annually.

Publications

EDA News is the newsletter of the European Dyslexia Association and is published three times a year. The newsletter provides information on current and future EDA activities as well as information on dyslexia-related events throughout Europe. Each issue also carries an introduction to one of our member organisations. *EDA News* is sent out to all EDA members, but is also available to individuals through our mailing service for a small annual subscription fee.

European Dyslexia Awareness Week

A few member organisations of the European Dyslexia Association, such as the British Dyslexia Association, currently organise an annual national Dyslexia Awareness Week. The week is devoted to media and public information campaigns. In an effort to support our members and to reflect European unity the EDA has proposed to its members the inauguration of a Europe-wide dyslexia awareness week. It is an opportunity to promote awareness of dyslexia and surrounding issues everywhere in Europe. In 2004, it was held from 27 September to 1 October. In 2005 it will be held from 3–8 October.

The Rights of Children with Dyslexia

EDA's vice-president, Professor Marta Bogdanowicz of the University of Gdansk, completed the task of compiling the results of an extensive questionnaire that she sent out to EDA's member associations. The object of this research was to gather ground level information on how the various policies of European governments directly affect children with dyslexia. Results of this survey were reported at the EDA conference and are also now published. This publication is a valuable overview of the current state of affairs and allows each country a chance to see how it compares with the rest of Europe.

The EDA Committee (from left to right)
Michael Kalmar (Osterreichischer Bundesverband Legasthenie, Austria)
Marta Bogdanowicz (Polskie Towarzystwo Dysleksje, Poland)
Susanne Bertschinger (Verband Dyslexie Schweiz, Switzerland)
Karin Brunger (Bundesverband Legasthenie e.V., Germany)
Teri Hegedus (Startdyslexia, Hungary)
H. Alan Sayles (Dyslexia Association of Ireland).

While there was a great deal of variation in the responses to the recognition of, and provision for, children with dyslexia, a few general conclusions can be noted here.

- Most countries represented by EDA membership have legislation concerning the fundamental rights of students with special educational needs, but rarely does this legislation mention specific conditions like dyslexia by name.
- Legislation rarely describes specific provision for people with dyslexia, but rather seeks to ensure rights to "appropriate" education for all those with disabilities and special educational needs. What is "appropriate" is never explained.

- Most countries are promoting inclusion for all children with special educational needs in mainstream schools.
- While most countries through policy or practice state that the first line of recognition and provision is dependent on the mainstream classroom teacher, the majority of teachers are not sufficiently knowledgeable in this area to fulfil this role.

While it is accepted that dyslexia is a condition inherent in the human species, it manifests itself mainly in confrontation with the educational demands of society. The overall effects of dyslexia depend on individual language systems and different educational methods, policies, and socio-cultural conditions. In dealing with dyslexia we must always remember that it is a practical problem involving real children. Dyslexia is not just a scientific riddle. There is an exceptional need for actual individualised help to be given to these children in the classroom. Legislation and educational policy must establish rights for these children to access an appropriate form of education that allows them to achieve their full potential regardless of their written language difficulties. This is a goal towards which EDA will continue to work.

International Dyslexia Association

J Thomas Viall, Executive Director

Brief History

The International Dyslexia Association (IDA) was founded in 1949 and has been serving individuals with dyslexia, their families and professionals in the field for more than fifty years. IDA was established to continue the pioneering work of Dr Samuel Torrey Orton, a neurologist who was one of the first to postulate the neurobiological basis of dyslexia. Along with Anna Gillingham and Bessie Stillman, he also worked to develop effective teaching approaches for individuals with dyslexia.

Since the founding of our organisation, many multisensory, structured, sequential systematic methods of language instruction have been developed based on Dr Orton's work. We proudly continue his philosophy that children with dyslexia can and should learn how to read. IDA receives no government support. We are funded through private donations, membership dues, foundation grants, sale of publications, conferences and other development efforts. IDA has just begun a "capital campaign" to purchase its own headquarters building which will serve as a true international centre for research, collaboration and distance learning. At the time of writing, more than US$1,500,000 have been donated to the project.

New Logo

In November 2004, the IDA Board of Directors approved a new logo for the organisation:

The was a strong sense that the new image is more modern and that it conveyes a celebratory feeling by styling the "X" to look represent a triumphant person.

The Membership

To fulfill our important mission, IDA has more than 13,500 active members in approximately 60 countries. IDA has 47 branches within North America and 4 National Affiliates (Brazil, the Czech Republic, Israel and the Philippines). Since our name change to The International Dyslexia Association in 1997, we are prudently expanding our international structure and outreach. We are currently considering plans to make the initiative more inclusive by eliminating all participation fees.

Our branches hold at least 4 public events per year (conferences, seminars, training sessions, parent and adult support groups etc). Branches also provide local information and referral services through networks with private and public schools, diagnosticians, tutors, physicians, researchers, parents and individuals with dyslexia. Our membership consists of people with dyslexia, professionals, and volunteers who work together for the benefit of individuals with dyslexia. Members receive:

- discounts on publications, conferences and workshops;
- subscription to our peer-reviewed journal 'Annals of Dyslexia' (now published twice annually);
- subscription to 'Perspectives' (a quarterly journal that focuses on a specific theme for each issue); and
- electronic member newsletter (twice annually).

The Services

In addition to membership and branch services, we offer information and referral services to the public. The headquarters of IDA is a clearing house of valuable information, responding to an average of 1500–2000 contacts during peak months. Our services include:

1 Free information on dyslexia (through Fact Sheets & reprinted articles from *Perspectives*) and access to a referral database that is "postal code" organised to locate the nearest resources for our consumers).

2 Our 4th generation website is "Bobby" certified (US based system to rate websites for accessibility to people with disabilities). The site contains free information on dyslexia, a new and more user friendly "Discussion Forum," links to other organisations, information on legislative activity, audio support, Spanish language resources and will soon be used for distance learning activities. The site can also be customized to viewer preferences (background color, font size, etc.). At peak times of the year, more than 70,000 people visit our site each month.

3 Many publications on dyslexia.

4 An annual international conference that brings together more than 3,000 experts in the field as well as individuals with dyslexia from more than 30 countries.

5 Funding for educational and medical research.

6 Participation in public awareness and public education initiatives.

7 Monitoring of, and lobbying for, federal legislation of interest to people with dyslexia.

8 Teacher preparation seminars as well as parent and adult support groups.

9 Legal advocacy to defend the rights of people with dyslexia. Recent successful lawsuits have ensured access to concessions for people with dyslexia when taking the Bar Exam and stopped discrimination against students who have accessed special arrangements when taking university entrance exams.

10 IDA has also adopted a 5 year plan to develop a national (USA) system to accredit specialised teacher training programmes and schools for students with learning disabilities. The "Alliance for Accreditation" will bring all the major accrediting and certifying organisations together in common purpose.

The Conferences

Our annual International Conference is attended by professionals and parents from around the world. It attracts more than 3,000 attendees from various disciplines. We also offer conference scholarships to teachers to expand the scope and impact of our conferences.

The Conferences are held all over the USA.

San Diego, California was the site of our 2003 conference. Dr Joseph Torgesen of the Florida Center for Reading Research (Florida State University) was the keynote speaker and Dr Patricia Kuhl of the University of Washington delivered the Norman Geschwind Memorial Lecture. Philadelphia, Pennsylvania (2004) and Denver, Colorado (2005), Indianapolis, Indiana (2006), and Dallas, Texas (2007) will host upcoming conferences.

Additionally, IDA co-sponsored, with the EDA and BDA, the Multilingualism and Dyslexia Conference (Manchester, UK, 1999). Continuing our collaboration with the BDA and EDA, the follow up conference, "Multilingual and Multicultural Perspectives on Dyslexia," was held in Washington DC in June, 2002. More than 500 people from around the world attended this critically important and cutting edge conference. IDA is collaborating with its colleagues in the European Dyslexia Association for the third conference in the series (to be held in Cyprus in 2005).

The Publications

IDA publishes many excellent materials, including The Orton Emeritus Series, a group of monographs dealing with the many issues relating to dyslexia and our position paper, "Informed Instruction for Reading Success: Foundations for Teacher Preparation". In addition, our quarterly journal, *Perspectives* follows a "theme issue" format; such topics as assistive technology, tips for parents, and controversial therapies have been covered in recent issues. Our flagship publication, *Annals of Dyslexia,* is one of the premier peer-reviewed journals published in the English language and is now published in two issues per year. Members of the BDA and EDA can also purchase *Annals* at the IDA member's discount of 20%. For information on our publications, please consult our online bookstore.

Vision

In its ongoing effort to "upgrade" programs and services, IDA has held a series of "Vision Retreats" over recent years. Our intent is to streamline the business components of the organisation to ensure financial stability while furthering our mission and purpose:

> *The purpose of IDA is to pursue and provide the most comprehensive range of information and services that address the full scope of dyslexia and related difficulties in learning to read and write...*
>
> *In a way that creates hope, possibility, and partnership...*
>
> *So that every individual has the opportunity to lead a productive and fulfilling life, and society benefits from the resource that is liberated.*

Contact Information

International Dyslexia Association
8600 LaSalle Road
Chester Building – Suite 382
Baltimore, MD 21286-2044
USA
Toll-free (US) (800) ABCD123
Tel: + 410 296 0232
Fax: + 410 321 5069
Website: www.interdys.org
General email: info@interdys.org

PATOSS

Louise Green, Committee Member

The Professional Association of Teachers of Students with Specific Learning Difficulties (PATOSS) is for all those concerned with the teaching and support of pupils with SpLD: dyslexic, dyspraxic, ADD, and Asperger's syndrome.

PATOSS was formed in 1987 as an association representing teachers who had gained the RSA (now OCR) Diploma for Teachers of Students with Specific Learning Difficulties. Since then, the number of PATOSS members has grown to over 1,000, working with students across the age range from primary through adult.

Since the OCR Diploma and Certificate courses were introduced, many other high quality training courses now exist and we are all aware of the importance of co-operation between professionals working to help children and adults with SpLD.

Membership is open to qualified teachers in SpLD and to those studying for either the certificate or the diploma in SpLD. PATOSS has widened its membership to include other professionals who are working in the field of specific learning difficulties.

Many of our members teach in schools and colleges. Many provide one-to-one tuition to students with specific learning difficulties. This includes assessment of current level of knowledge and ability, planning programmes of work, delivering those programmes, advising on the broader educational programme, and liaising with other professionals.

We provide a range of services to our members. We welcome new members and hope that you will apply to join.

PATOSS aims:

- to establish and maintain the professional status of those qualified to teach students with specific learning difficulties;
- to promote the continued provision and development of appropriate specialist qualifications in the teaching of students with SpLD;
- to enable members to update and extend their knowledge and skills and to exchange ideas through an annual conference, bulletins and local groups;
- to promote fuller understanding and recognition of SpLD;

- to promote links with teachers working with SpLD students in all sectors of education;
- to promote links with other professionals involved in the field of SpLD;
- to give a professional corporate response to the Department for Education and Skills (DfES) on matters affecting SpLD students; and
- to maintain a register of the members of the association.

PATOSS offers:

- links with other professionals;
- opportunities to keep in touch with recent research and to exchange knowledge and experience;
- a range of publications;
- reduced fees for PATOSS national conferences and local events;
- a growing network of local groups; and
- different levels of insurance including professional indemnity.

PATOSS has been a supporting corporate member of the BDA for many years and I am also currently Chair of the Supporting Corporate Members' Committee. We also have PATOSS representatives on a DfES working party for assessment in further and higher education and on the General Teachers' Council. We are looking to work in closer partnership with BDA.

More details about PATOSS as well as various information sheets can be found on the PATOSS website: www.patoss-dyslexia.org.

CReSTeD (Council for the Registration of Schools Teaching Dyslexic pupils)

Dr Michael Cane, Chairman

Brief History

The Council for the Registration of Schools Teaching Dyslexic pupils is a charity set up to provide some guidance and reassurance to parents who are seeking a school for their dyslexic child. The CReSTeD Register of schools is provided, free of charge, to parents.

CReSTeD is committed to improving the standards of provision for dyslexic pupils. Increasingly parents are looking to the CReSTeD Register as the first stage in their search for a suitable school.

Schools who apply to go on the CReSTeD Register are subject to a visit by one or two CReSTeD consultants (depending on the level of provision offered). Unlike many other lists of schools offering help for dyslexia, the CReSTeD Register consists of schools whose provision has been evaluated by consultants and then appraised by CReSTeD's pre-registration committee of experienced Heads. Therefore, the register gives a level of reassurance for parents which, at the least, should save them some time in selecting a short list of schools for their child. The Register is updated twice a year and the website is constantly updated.

Pupils and Dyslexia

No two dyslexic individuals are the same. They show individual variations in abilities, attitudes and difficulties and thus differ in their special educational needs. No single pattern of provision is going to be appropriate for all students who are dyslexic. CReSTeD recognises this important fact and has structured its Register to show four different categories of provision in schools. Obviously there is a continuous spectrum of needs but the use of four categories seems to give a manageable range of levels of provision. One of the key aims of CReSTeD is to help the parent find provision which matches the needs of their child. This appropriate provision may be in a mainstream school with support or it may be in a special school.

The Categories

Category SP: These schools specialise in dyslexic students whose difficulties are usually of marked severity. These students require provision throughout the whole curriculum and may also need input for the loss of self confidence and self esteem as a consequence of their learning problems. This special environment can help by removing the constant adverse comparisons with their non dyslexic peers.

Category SP schools are usually small in size, with small classes, offering as broad and balanced a curriculum as is commensurate with the stated aims of the school. All teaching in all classes should be adjusted to the learning needs of the pupil.

Category DU: These schools are usually larger and offer specialist dyslexia education to a proportion of the school's

population. Usually the majority of learning takes place in an ordinary classroom setting. Special input, usually for difficulties with aspects of (English) language and possibly mathematics, takes place in a unit. The unit often offers support for other aspects of the curriculum and will co-ordinate input with the rest of the school.

Category SC: These schools meet the needs of their dyslexic students within ordinary classrooms, using special tuition within the classroom setting rather than in a unit. The school can usually call on outside experts (psychologists, support services etc) if needed. All teachers should have a good and active awareness of the difficulties dyslexic pupils experience.

Category WS: These schools offer a full curriculum which the dyslexic student should be largely able to follow and deal with independently. Special input is offered by withdrawal to work with a specialist teacher usually during the normal school day. Again, it would be expected that all teachers in the school are aware of, and acknowledge, the needs of pupils who are dyslexic.

Re-registration

Schools must renew their registration every three years. This requires a visit by a CReSTeD consultant. During their registration period, schools are expected to notify CReSTeD if there are any significant changes, including change of ownership, new Head or new specialist teacher. These changes may result in an interim visit from a consultant. This frequency of re-registration is one of the shortest of any organisation.

CReSTeD can also initiate a "Responsive Visit" to a school using one of its consultants if it has particular concerns.

Parents' Checklist

This list, published in the back of the Register suggests twenty-three points to consider when answering the six key questions:

1 How suitable is the school's policy and structure?

2 How appropriate are the buildings and resources?

3 How sympathetic and aware are the staff?

4 How knowledgeable and well trained are the staff in understanding and providing for the education of dyslexic pupils?

5 How suitable and accessible is the general curriculum?

6 How detailed and individually appropriate is the special provision?

Parents should be aware that, for a school to be on the CReSTeD Register, it is not just a matter of paying a registration fee. The criteria are there to be met. Council can and does remove schools from the Register. It does refuse to list schools.

The CReSTeD Register can be obtained by contacting the CReSTeD Administrator:
Email: admin@crested.org.uk
Tel: 00 44 (0)1242 604 852
Web: www.crested.org.uk

Smaller Dyslexia Organisations

There are many dyslexia organisations, many of whom work at a national level and are well known. Some of them have written about their activities in this Handbook. This year we are launching a new section to profile some of the smaller, less well known ones who tend to concentrate at a regional level. In subsequent editions of the Handbook we will concentrate on different organisations each time, in order to give you a flavour of the excellent sterling work that is done in the field.

For this issue let us introduce:

- The Arts Dyslexia Trust.
- Cumbria County Co-ordinating Group on Dyslexia.
- Dyslexia Advice and Resource Centre (DARC), Birmingham.

We hope you enjoy reading about their activities.

Susan Tresman and Ann Cooke
Editors

Arts Dyslexia Trust – A Brief History

Susan Parkinson, Chief Executive and Secretary

The Arts Dyslexia Trust (ADT) was established in 1992 but its history really goes back much further than that, back to the early '60s when the word 'dyslexia' was scarcely known in England. A remarkable small independent school (Brickwall in Sussex) run by a very remarkable headmaster, Malcolm Ritchie, was one of the first in England to recognise dyslexia. He attempted to build up a group of teaching staff who could meet the learning needs of young dyslexic minds. I was fortunate enough to be asked to join this group and became responsible for art classes for the next 20 years.

As soon as I arrived I became fascinated by the work that was being created by the boys in these classes. Compared with the work produced in the art colleges where I had previously been teaching, their creative imagination was simply outstanding and the results amazing. This was in spite of a severe lack of equipment and inadequate space – the art room was a dark and subterranean ex-cowshed with a chronically uneven brick floor. I remember watching anxiously as snow flakes drifted down through the unsealed roof on to the heads of the visiting inspectors! Fortunately they didn't notice!

By the time I retired in 1985 I had become convinced that there must be some reason why a lack of ability with words should so often bring with it a higher than average ability in subjects requiring visual-spatial skills. I took a degree course in Research Methods with the Open University, determined to discover the roots of this connection. Of course I was always being told that this connection did not exist but I soon found that the evidence was there. From research by Norman Geschwind, Albert Galaburda and many others, I gathered the clues to the explanation I was looking for.

To sum up the conclusions very briefly, I believe that traditional academic education depends on the use of words and numbers which can only be understood sequentially. The visual thinkers, including many of the talented dyslexics, think three dimensionally. The differences between these two ways of thinking are profound. They affect all sorts of things, not only the way people learn. I have written several papers on the subject and would be happy to send one to any reader who is interested.

One major source of misunderstanding is that it is not generally appreciated that there are two ways of perceiving, recording and manipulating visual information in your brain: two-dimensionally (i.e. as flat pattern) and three-dimensionally. It is the latter form which is most commonly used by dyslexic people. The fact that none of the so-called "visual" tests distinguish between these two ways of thinking and very, very few are presented in three-dimensional formats, explains perhaps why there is such controversy on the subject and why there are still so many people who refuse to believe that the dyslexic visual talent exists.

When the Trust was formed the first thing we did was to mount a big exhibition to demonstrate this dyslexic talent. It attracted enormous support from the art world and elsewhere. Richard Rogers lent us some of his beautiful architectural models, we showed Leonardo prints from the

Queen's collection at Windsor, pages from Faraday's illustrated notebooks, extracts from Einstein's mathematical notes and a beautiful photograph of one of Yeats's handwritten poems kindly given to us by the current editor of his letters. "A first exhibition of its kind" was welcomed by Sir Richard de Grey, the President of the Royal Academy, in his foreword in the exhibition catalogue. He hoped that those responsible for education policy "would take note". Alas, it seems even now they still have not taken note.

One special feature of the exhibition was the illustrated talks given by Thomas West. These were an inspiration and eye opener to many. ADT were the first people to invite him over to England after the publication of his book *In the Mind's Eye*. Since then he has been a much sought after speaker at many conferences on dyslexia in the UK.

From this promising start the ADT has gone on to give help to numerous young dyslexic people seeking university courses and to older professional artists wanting opportunities to develop and/or show their work. Not surprisingly in our word based society, the BDA, Dyslexia Institute and other dyslexia help groups had been concentrating solely on providing remedial assistance for the literacy problems encountered by dyslexic people. There was little knowledgeable source of guidance and encouragement for the strengths of talented dyslexic people, including mature adults who were suddenly discovering late in life their own dyslexic tendencies via the assessment and reports on their children and grandchildren.

It was in order to fill this perceived gap in provision that the ADT was founded. We gathered together experts in the main disciplines of the arts who, being dyslexic themselves, could easily relate to those experiencing the same obstacles and antagonisms that they had encountered on their own way to success. Although visual-spatial ability is most obviously apparent in the visual arts, it is also an important factor in the sciences and in all fields involving creative work. Therefore our advisers need to cover these fields too. From the original founders (three teachers, all from Brickwall) the ADT has grown to include musicians, dancers, actors, businessmen, sportsmen, computer buffs, poets and so on.

Long may the creative dyslexic mind flourish!

If you would like further information on the Arts Dyslexia Trust and a copy of their catalogue, please contact:

Arts Dyslexia Trust
Lodge Cottage
Brabourne Lees
Ashford
Kent
TN25 6QZ
Tel/Fax: 01303 813 221
Email: artsdyst@aol.com

Darkness embraces us

Jon Adams

We lay, with legs entwined
Darkness embracing us
As tree roots binding Roman amphorae,
Abandoned.
Buried.
Still holding their treasured secrets,
Splintering with ever increasing seasons growth.

Tarnished silver.
Cimmerian knights,
Awaiting betrayal with every new dawn.
An ever pressing crowd,
Cheering Diocletians games
In their own private coliseum.

Long after their dark embraced burial
Abandoned talents,
   banished servant
Awaiting repayment fourfold.
Cold blue digging,
With fevered backward glances
Bleeding hands smooth the red earth
Waiting to rush into eternity.

We lay, with legs entwined
Darkness embracing us
Stripped bare,
Still,
Fallen, by passions storm.

Cumbria County Co-ordinating Group on Dyslexia

Heather Swain, Educational Psychologist and Chair of Cumbria County Coordinating Group

Why Does Cumbria Need a Co-ordinating Group?

Cumbria's County Co-ordinating Group on Dyslexia was formed in the early 1990s. The aim was to bring together individuals and groups in the county who had an interest in meeting the needs of dyslexic children and adults.

Cumbria is a beautiful, mostly rural county, but it is also vast. There are currently three local Dyslexia Associations based in the South, the West and the North of the county. Each of these associations has its own membership and committee. The Co-ordinating Group acts as a welcome forum for these three groups to meet with a range of other organisations.

Who is Part of the Co-ordinating Group?

The County Co-ordinating Group is open to anyone, and people can and do just turn up for meetings, often when they have an issue they need support with.

Alongside members of the local dyslexia associations, other organisations represented include:

- specialist teachers of children with literacy difficulties, including both those working for the Education Authority and those working for other organisations;
- representatives from the local Certificate in Specific Learning Difficulties course, accredited by Bangor University and the BDA;
- educational psychologists and inspectors/advisers from the Education Service;
- parent partnership workers;
- Connexions staff and tutors from local colleges;
- an adult dyslexia officer; and
- library and Heritage Services staff.

What About the Practicalities?

The group meets three times each year. Meetings are held in different areas of the county, to try to make it possible for everyone to attend at some point.

The group has a co-ordinator who organises venues, an agenda and the distribution of minutes. The minimal costs of servicing the group are met by Cumbria Education Service, and by the generosity of local colleges and other organisations that provide venues free of charge.

But What Does the Group Actually Do?

Anyone who is part of the group can contribute to the agenda. A particularly valued standing agenda item is an 'update' section where those present can give feedback about particular successes they have had, or provide information about forthcoming events. The group also:

- offers informal opportunities for networking;
- allows people to meet to request help with projects and to plan joint events;
- discusses recent research and developments in the field of dyslexia;
- invites external speakers to talk informally on topics of particular interest, especially those with direct implications for local policy and practice;
- provides an opportunity for people to ask questions and request information;
- listens to, and tries to find a way of resolving concerns that are brought by members; and
- provides feedback on proposed developments in policy and practice.

At the 2004 BDA International Conference held at the University of Warwick, Professor Rod Nicholson stressed the importance of all parts of the dyslexia 'ecosystem' working together to move forward. Cumbria's County Co-ordinating Group is a practical way of achieving such 'working together' for the benefit of children and adults with dyslexia across the county.

Dyslexia Advice and Resource Centre (DARC)

Lynn Mason, DARC Volunteer

The Dyslexia Advice and Resource Centre (DARC) in Birmingham is a registered charity and company limited by guarantee. We work as a non-profit making organisation. Our aim is to provide professional expertise, information and support to individuals with dyslexia in terms of their personal development and in finding and sustaining employment. Above all, our aim is to ensure a better quality of life for those affected by dyslexia at all levels.

We have a wide client group, ranging from individuals requiring 'one to one' support, to providing advice and assistance to companies, employment services, colleges and schools. Our specialist work, related to young people aged 14 years and above, is delivered through an alternative curriculum programme. The programme, specifically designed to cater for those youngsters who may have been excluded or who are in danger of being excluded from school, is about raising self esteem and motivation and turning them back on to learning. The course supports the individual to develop their own personal strategies to cope with the day to day difficulties posed by their dyslexia, and to approach challenges in a more constructive and positive way.

Over the years DARC has also had the opportunity to support people in the workplace. A prime example of this has been supporting employees from the West Midlands Emergency Services. This work has included initial identification of dyslexia, the development of learning strategies, awareness-raising amongst employers and the development of a Dyslexic Recruitment Policy. In recognition of the support received and services provided, DARC was recently presented with a painting featuring the flight of an Air Ambulance in acknowledgement for the 'outstanding' support given to dyslexic colleagues across the services.

DARC was formed by a group of adult dyslexics in Birmingham in 1997. Frustrated by their dyslexia and keen to find an alternative approach to their difficulties other than basic skills provision, the group sought out alternative approaches to address their needs. The solution was to develop the 'Learning to Succeed' programme. The programme, developed by dyslexics for dyslexics, is an innovative and successful programme designed to focus on building skills and strategies to cope with dyslexia in everyday life. The aim is to give dyslexics more control over the results they produce in their lives and through this process enable them to participate in many training and educational opportunities that might otherwise be unavailable to them. The course has been delivered to over 4,000 people over the last seven years and has had an amazing impact upon people's lives. Comments from participants have included:

> *"It was a fantastic course that has been life changing for me! It was very helpful to me in all kinds of ways. I feel better about tackling things that I would have walked away from before and I know feel empowered to go to do things in my life, like more studying and helping my kids with their schoolwork"*

"The best part of the course was sharing my experiences with people who understand what I have been through and finding ways to succeed with the things I've always wanted to do".

The course has an achievement rate of 97%. It is currently being delivered across the UK, Australia, New Zealand and Europe and is being translated for delivery in Germany.

DARC continues to be managed and run by dyslexics and its vision has not altered since those early days in wanting to find effective methods of supporting and providing information, resources and training for young people and adults with dyslexia in the West Midlands. Our services now include:

- a confidential helpline – currently taking over 10,000 phone calls a year;
- a dyslexia screening service;
- advice & guidance – DARC has recently been awarded the Matrix IAG (Information Advice & Guidance) Quality Kitemark;
- dyslexia awareness training sessions – delivered throughout the year across the West Midlands and as far afield as Cornwall, Brighton, and London;
- advice service to organisations – DARC works with a wide range of organisations to assist them to become more dyslexia-friendly;
- delivery of the 'Learning to Succeed' programme. This course is currently being delivered across the country in a variety of locations including prisons, young offender's institutions, colleges and schools;
- Training the Trainers. DARC provides a training course to teachers and tutors wishing to deliver the 'Learning to Succeed' programme;

- research – DARC has been involved in a recent study to investigate the incidence of dyslexia amongst employees in the creative industries sector.

Recent Publications

- Dyslexia, Learning to Succeed – DARC's Experience. Fox-Kirk, W. & Crawley, S. (2003). Published by DARC, Birmingham.
- Dyslexia and Core Skills for Foyers and Hostel Clients. Crawley, S (2000). Published by Learn Link Research and Development, Birmingham
- Dyslexia and the Creative Industries. Rose, S. & Taylor, J. (2004). Published by Birmingham Learning and Skills Council & the European Commission

All of the above publications are available from DARC.

For further information contact:

Dyslexia Advice and Resource Centre Limited
The Toll House
The Bond
180–182 Fazeley Street
Digbeth
Birmingham
B5 5SE
Tel: 0121 248 2429
Email: admin@darcweb.co.uk

We Succeed

A tribute to Steve Rose, tutor and creator of the programme "Learning to Succeed" for dyslexic adults

We succeed moving from the thorn.
Creating a sensation, which uses imagination.
Like the matrix, I'll show you the door, you will have to walk through it...

We started with 10, but now ending with 8,
The movement in our minds we appreciate.

The Rose, he really made the difference.
Moving us from Confusion 2 Resolution,
Destitution 2 Habitation.

Our Minds... Breathing.
Our Minds... He Rejuvenates! Motivates!
Invigorates and accelerates up the stem from thorn, to the soft, sweet leafy flowerbed, the colour dawn...

Our Minds... Breathing.
Being at ease, ready to succeed.

Dyslexia is very good, very beautiful.
Just like a field of rose.

Our Mind... Rejuvenated! Motived! Invigorated.
Empowered by Learning to Succeed.

Shawna Beecher

Shawna Beecher can be contacted on 07949 754 904

Part 2

Managing Dyslexia in Children and Young People

How Dyslexia Affects Musicians (and some strategies)

John Westcombe, Chair of the BDA Music Committee

The following exchange took place several years ago at a youth orchestra audition:

Smartly presented trombonist says that he is to play *Sophisticated Lady* by Ben Elton. Music adviser gently suggests that he has the wrong composer. Candidate looks in music and says,

"Sorry, I am going to play *Sophisticated Lady* by Elton John". Asked whether it might actually be by Duke Ellington, the trombonist looks in his music again and says, in a perfect put down,

"You're right. If you knew that in the first place why didn't you tell me?"

I was the adviser involved, and have told this story elsewhere, but it seems to reveal a number of points. Regrettably, only some time afterwards did I realise that the lad probably had dyslexic traits. He was reading inaccurately, was mildly challenged when he wasn't expecting it and, critically, had mixed up his syllables. We didn't enquire whether he found reading music difficult, and invited him to join. It's important to log the notion of success early in this article!

The struggle for recognition of dyslexia in general has its parallel in music. The early pioneers like Violet Brand, Margaret Hubicki and Tim Miles had to work hard to get acceptance. Examination boards (not only in music of course) now allow special considerations for sight reading. The steady course of awareness raising has meant that many teachers, having recognised pupils with the well known traits, such as sequencing weakness, have already amended their teaching methods. As expected, the reading of notation is a prominent hurdle and we are familiar with the panic-under-pressure problem. The delay in processing and acquiring automaticity of response can lead to the cry, in respect of a known piece: 'It feels like sight reading every time I look at it'.

Naturally, these requirements in music relate to memory – both in attempting to play or sing back short fragments (and possibly playing a short tune correctly but not realising that it's a well known tune) and, from another angle, securing lines of music in the 'bank'. This last one is essential for opera solo singers who cannot have their music on stage. So there's a lot involved in the 'doing' of music – although we might cede, in memorising and doing a couple of other things, to the simultaneous translators at the United Nations!

There is also a sense of needing to bring to bear five aspects:

- the notes;
- the eye;
- the brain;
- the finger work; and
- the control of resultant sound.

The first two are omitted in improvisation of course, and a huge amount of joyful music-making goes on without notation, notably in jazz. Young classroom composers can leave directions for their successors without them being in 5-line stave notation.

Organisational matters may need attention: the right room, having the right music and place on the visiting teacher's rota. Laterality needs to be considered. Some pupils find it easier if the teacher (pointing) says 'play (x) with this hand and (y) with that hand' rather than name the hands. Sometimes simply going back to the left hand side of the page and a new line can cause trouble; green and red markings can help (as can highlighting a pattern which repeats elsewhere.)

There is an attempted strategy which I call 'camouflage', where the pupil presents as having made some progress but with odd errors. Probably he/she has tried to memorise, to avoid working out the notation each time, and done so inaccurately, but appears to be reading the music. Teachers Beware! (Incidentally, it may be wise for a young person with dyslexic traits to start on a single line instrument rather than the piano; there's a lot to master, and some are really foxed by the chords appearing vertical and the keyboard horizontal.)

Some traits will stay with musicians into the profession – those who succeed will have worked very hard indeed, but there are many successes and there is satisfaction in devising strategies.

Slowness in processing means very hard work in preparation, but those teachers who have worked systematically and 'brick by brick' are forever lauded. Singers with these traits will have few worries when rehearsals stretch over two or three months, such as the chorus in professional opera, as there are various methods of internalising the vocal lines e.g. from CDs etc. However, in asserting that, the Chorus Director of the Royal Opera

House, Covent Garden added that they would struggle in the 'session' world, where a lot of music is recorded within 3 hours of starting, often at sight and in different languages. There may also be hazards in accepting short-notice deputising work.

We shouldn't assume anything when helping folk with dyslexic traits. In particular we should not assume that concepts of rhyme and high-low have been understood.

- In the case of the latter, watch an infants class doing movement. Two or three pupils are watching what the others do on the high-low front and are copying.
- In another context, one pupil made no progress on the piano until it was realised that she thought the note on the stave to be played was where the stalk stopped at the other end, not where the blob was!

Music's conventions don't help:

- The music page is very crowded, with important directions often being tiny.
- For some people the music lines go watery – 'like a rock-pool'.
- The time signature looks like a fraction but isn't.
- A potential difficulty known in other contexts – the looking up and down from the white-board to the classroom desk – occurs when players need to look at the conductor and then at their music while processing all sorts of other things.
- Percussionists need to move around between instruments and music stands.

Instrument construction has its inconsistencies – half the string instruments work one way, the rest the other. There's a multisensory point here; if the cellist wishes to raise the pitch, the controlling hand goes away from the body. If a violinist wishes to do so, the hand comes towards the body.

Successes and Strategies

In all this there are many pluses to be celebrated. Sometimes dyslexic traits bring with them creative minds, with right-brain strengths. Sometimes they see a piece as a whole, where others cannot grasp that aspect. They may be better at pitch and tonality and possibly less good at rhythm. (Early on, this often shows through inability to keep a steady beat). Choir training is very beneficial, through the required separation of syllables and the importance of clear pronunciation. Music can now be composed via sound-creation and 'play and print' technologies, often removing the pen and paper requirement.

Strategies also include eternal patience, particularly when someone wants to return to the opening every time a mistake is made, or is 'stuck'. Others include:

- the teacher's encouragement of improvisation;
- duetting;
- recording work in progress;
- playing alongside not opposite;
- writing useful clues on the music; and
- analysing pupils' learning styles.

Teaching to the pupil's strengths naturally follows. My colleague, Sheila Oglethorpe, favours a small frame whose window on the page allows concentration on perhaps two or three bars of difficulty, with all other information blocked out, and also a tactic of a 'short break' in the lesson. Some teachers, and physicist parents, find that the recurrence of the A-G letter pattern can be explained by citing the beautiful physical properties which underline the octave, e.g., one A sounds at 220 cycles per second, the next one up at 440 cps. The keyboard underlines this patterning. Going on to HIJK wouldn't work.

Music can help us all with alphabet and tables; its patterns and rhythms help those with dyslexic traits even more so in aspects of memory and timing. There is some evidence that learning music can assist in more general remediation.

Back to the bugbear – notation. We have to recognise it for what it is. For hundreds of years it was paramount, but now, so much music can be improvised without it, in classroom, cathedral organ loft, Ronnie Scott's and the Asian music ensemble. Indeed, rappers are part of that society! An improvisation day conference for those groups? Wow!

Alongside this, the advances in research on the brain promise well, particularly in what the brain is doing while music is being learned. There is still much to be done in seeking firm evidence of the incidence of dyslexia amongst the various sectors of the musical fraternity.

Yes, dyslexia does hinder some musicians, but determination, and thoughtful, wide-angled multisensory teaching, goes a long way towards minimising the difficulties.

Further Reading

Dyslexia, temporal processing and Music; the potential of music as an early learning aid for dyslexic children. Katie Overy, 2000. Psychology of Music, Vol.28 No.2

PATOSS Bulletin, 2003. Volume 16 No.3

Instrumental music for dyslexics (second edition). Oglethorpe, S, 2002. Whurr Publishers.

Music and dyslexia – opening new doors. Miles, T. R. and Westcombe, J. (Eds), 2001. Whurr Publishers

Books for Dyslexic Readers

Janet Hatcher, Dyslexia Institute

Many children with dyslexic difficulties need help to develop their word attack skills at the word and sentence level. They may follow a structured programme that is multi-sensory and moves in small steps. As well as this, however, children with literacy difficulties need to have lots of practice in using their decoding skills whilst reading books.

Background Research

The Dyslexia Institute recently undertook a research project (Rack and Hatcher, 2002) that looked at ways in which parents can help to support their children's reading. One of the things we found was that, in addition to developing firm foundations in alphabetic skills, children are helped by applying these skills when reading books. Lots of other research (Hatcher, 2000, Torgesen et al. 2001) also shows that including text reading in an intervention programme leads to improved reading.

Based on the evidence from the research, the Dyslexia Institute produced the DIY Readers' Support Pack for Parents. This pack includes guidelines on how parents can help children with reading books. However, parents and carers want to know what kinds of books they can use.

Choosing Books

When parents are selecting a book they might ask four questions:

1 What type of reading is the book suitable for?

2 Is the book at the right level for the type of reading?

3 Is the book presented in a dyslexia friendly way?

4 Where can I get further help?

What type of reading is the book suitable for?
Clearly, how a child approaches a book that they will find easy to read is quite different from approaching a book that they will find more difficult. Parents need to decide whether they are going to read out loud to their child, whether the child will read the book, or whether reading will be shared. The choice of book will, therefore, be governed by what kind of reading is intended. Where it is intended that a child reads the book without support, then the level of difficulty of the book is very important.

Is the book at the right level?

When children are practising their word skills and reading strategies, it is important that the book they are reading is at the right level of text reading difficulty. It is generally recognised that when children read books at the instructional level they should be reading with about 90 to 94% accuracy. If the reading age of the book is known (as, for example in the Waterstones Guide to Books for Young Dyslexic Readers), then it is easier to make a good match with the child's reading age. However, often this is not possible. In that case, a useful, approximate, 'trick' that can be used is the five-finger test:

- Choose a page that is representative of the book.
- As the child reads the page, he/she should put up one finger each time a word cannot be read accurately.
- If 5 fingers are put up before the page is completed the book is likely to be too hard.

When thinking about the readability of a book, a number of other characteristics can also be considered. These are the kind of criteria that are used for grading books into book levels.

- Is there a clear relationship between the text and the pictures? For children in the early stages of reading it is very important that clues to reading the words can be found in the pictures.
- How many sentences are there to a page of writing? Look for shorter sentences. Over 15 words in a sentence means that the sentence is becoming complex.
- Are there lots of words with more than 6 letters? Words over this length can become much harder to decode as they have more syllables.
- Is the grammatical structure of the sentences simple? A large number of changes of tense (as often happens with dialogue), contractions (such as *I'm, don't*) and negatives makes the text harder to read and comprehend.

Book Presentation and Storyline
Children who are finding it difficult to learn to read often use up a lot of their 'thinking' time on working out what the words are (decoding) and have little time left for thinking about the content of the text. They might also approach the task of reading in a very passive way, by ignoring words or by letting others tell them words, so doing the 'reading' work for them. How a book is presented and the clarity of the story can make a difference to comprehension.

Try to select books:

- that are attractive;
- that are well illustrated;
- where the print is clearly set out;
- that have a straightforward storyline and strong characters; and
- where the chapters are short and the overall length of the book is manageable.

Some examples

- *The Very Hungry Caterpillar* by Eric Carle (reading age: 6;10), makes very imaginative use of illustration.
- *Where's Spot?* By Eric Hill (reading age: 6;4) helps to associate books with having fun
- Ladybird publish a wide range of 'Learn to Read' books:
  - The 'Read It Yourself' books (e.g. *Snow White and the Seven Dwarfs – level 4* – reading age: 7;4) can help children to increase the bank of high frequency words that they know.
  - The 'Phonics' range (e.g. *The Ghost House* – reading age: 7;0) help children to practise the links between letters and sounds.

- The Jumpstart series published by Collins (e.g. *Active Earth* – reading age: 7;0) have simple short text and illustrations or photographs on every page.
- As well as being a well established structured reading scheme, Oxford Reading Tree is adding more titles to its main 'trunk' and 'branches'. For example the *Wolf Hill Series* provides graded books that are suitable for children with dyslexia
- For older pupils there are many popular books, by well known authors, with very strong story lines but accessible text:
  - *Connie and the Waterbabies* by Jacqueline Wilson (reading age: 8;2)
  - *The Twits* by Roald Dahl (reading age: 9;3+)
  - *The Diary of a Killer Cat* by Anne Fine (reading age: 8;0)
  - *Horrid Henry* by Francesca Simon (reading age: 8;6)

Where can I get further help?

- Libraries go out of their way to encourage children to take pleasure from books. Many libraries run special activities, or have regular story time and reading clubs.
- The Waterstones Guide to Books for Young Dyslexic Readers recommends over 100 titles together with similar books from many well known series such as *Barrington Stoke, Dead Famous,* and *Super Crunchies.*
- The DIY Pack provides information on how parents can help children with reading. It describes games and activities that are linked to books, so that children can revisit words many times in different contexts
- The Dyslexia Institute website (www.dyslexia-inst.org.uk) includes information on how to grade books, together with an extensive book list of finely graded books (to be found under 'Publications and News').

- More information on grading books can be found in a *Special* article, *Making the Grades* (Hatcher, 2004)

References

Hatcher, J. (2004) 'Making the Grades' in *Special – Supporting and Developing Good Practice,* NASEN

Hatcher, P.J. (2000 b) *Sound Linkage: An Integrated Programme for Overcoming Reading Difficulties 2nd Edition.* London, Whurr

Rack, J. and Hatcher, J. (2002) *SPELLIT: An Overview of the Project.* Dyslexia Review Vol 14 number 1

Torgesen, J.K., Alexander, A.W., Wagner, R.K., Rashotte,K.S.V. and Conway, T. (2001). Intensive Remedial Instruction for Children with Severe Reading Disabilities: Immediate and Long-term Outcomes from Two Instructional Approaches. Journal of Learning Disabilities,34(1), 33–58,78.

Resources

Dyslexia Institute (2002) *The Dyslexia Institute Young Readers' Support Pack for Parents*

Game for Anything

Bob Hext, Crossbow Education Limited

As well as assisting with learning, playing games at home can help develop a wide range of social, thinking and memory skills and create opportunities for success that are particularly important for dyslexic children who may be struggling in school.

Before I started working with dyslexic children in 1988, I was a French teacher. The French phrase for board games is "jeux de société", which translates as "social games". In our high speed, hi-tech world traditional family entertainment such as sitting down together to play cards or board games is disappearing from view. With them a raft of valuable social skills are disappearing too, such as taking turns, patience, tolerance, having the right attitude to winning and losing, self control and communication skills, attention, concentration, memory and a whole range of visual and auditory skills which are particularly valuable for dyslexic children. By ignoring "social games" we are closing down one of life's important training grounds.

Probably the most valuable commercially available game resource a family can possess is a pack of cards. If you don't know any card games, you can buy several books for about £5 that will teach you as many games as you need to know. Buy a couple of packs of playing cards while you are there. If you don't know where to start with ordinary playing cards, take a slightly different track and go and buy a pack of **Uno**. You won't regret trying that.

Not only does a card game meet all the criteria for "social games", but young children can learn and practise foundation mathematical skills, such as counting, sequencing and recognising clusters of "pips" as different numbers. A simple game of **Pairs** is good for visual memory. **Go Fish** and **Happy Families** develop auditory memory, while **Rummy** combines memory with reasoning ("I've just picked up a 6. I remember she discarded one a few turns back. Therefore she might discard another one and that will give me a set"). Trumping games such as **Whist** are excellent for memory and attention. Our favourite family card game is called **Racing Demon**. I cannot go into detail here but the rules can be found on our website at www.crossboweducation.com. It's the best game I know for speed, visual attention and concentration.

We have played cards, and Racing Demon in particular, with all our children, certainly, in the case of the two youngest, since before they started school. My eldest daughter who is dyslexic was being given secondary maths work by the time she was in Year 4. She is now at university studying medicine. Our middle daughter was two books ahead of her peers in the infants and, in Year 8, was being called "an outstanding mathematician" by her maths teacher. Our youngest was also streets ahead at primary school. She got level 5 at Key Stage 2 SATs and maths is now her best subject. Since neither my wife not myself are particularly strong mathematicians, I suggest that all their hours spent playing cards have had an effect.

For all the commercial games available, you often can't do better than some of the old standards. For pure reasoning combined with the right amount of luck and guesswork to make it sufficiently unpredictable, I don't think you can beat **Master Mind**. Compact and inexpensive, it is a great idea for a stocking filler at Christmas. Like many other games, Master Mind can also be played online. Other perennials that are excellent for strategy and reasoning are **Rumikub, Othello** and **Draughts**. These are two-player games and, as such, provide you with the opportunity of giving a child some exclusive attention for the duration of the game. There will be emotional benefits alongside the cognitive skills gained.

The best games are often the simplest. One of the simplest and best is Rummy. It is an excellent game for adapting because the point of the game is to collect sets and much learning also involves sets. Basic Rummy is played as follows:

- 7 cards are dealt to each player; the remainder are placed faced down in the centre.
- The top card from the pack is turned up and left next to the pack (starting the "discard" pile).
- Players must collect two sets of cards, which can either be 3-4 card **of the same suit** in sequence or 3-4 cards **of the same value** in different suits.
- Players take turns to pick up one card at a time, either from the top of the unseen pack or from the top of the discard pile.
- Players must also discard one card at each turn, which can either be the card that they have just picked up or another card from their hand.
- Through this selection process players alter their hands until the winner lays down all his cards, discarding the last one.

So now you can play Rummy (reasoning, memory, communication, social skills etc). Try adapting this for learning specific sets, play with just four cards to make one set instead of two. Choose four colours for your four suits. On the cards you write spelling families, topic vocabulary or whatever needs to be learnt. To make a winning set you need one word in all four colours or all four words of one colour. You can add a further memory element to the game: instead of just putting the winning cards down, the winning player must place them **face down** on the table for one complete round, then repeat (or spell) them from memory before turning them over. He only wins the game if he gets them right, otherwise he must change his cards. Anxiety shuts down thinking. To a dyslexic child who experiences failure and frustration on a daily basis the anxiety response is practically automatic when the word "remember" is mentioned. To set a memory task in the risk free context of a card game can help to bypass that anxiety trigger and get the brain remembering.

You can find games all around you:

- Move a few objects in the living room while your children are out of the room and see if they can "spot the difference" (visual memory).
- Play "I went on holiday and I took . . . " on car journeys (auditory memory).
- See how many words you can make beginning with P in 30 seconds (processing speed).
- Play 20 questions (verbal reasoning).
- Bingo and pairs have a thousand faces and all of them wear a smile.

I have a weak back and need to do regular exercises so that my backbone has sufficient muscular support. The exercises bear little resemblance to walking. Lately I have been ignoring my exercises ("too busy!"). Two days ago my back gave way and today I am walking with two sticks. These games are like my exercises: they bear little resemblance to the activities they support but we ignore them at our cost.

Box Hext is the founder of Crossbow Education. He lectures widely on the use of games and puzzles for teaching. For training enquiries please contact 01785 660902 or email bob@crossboweducation.com.

Dyslexia and Outdoor Learning

Mary Twomey

The opportunity to develop skills in outdoor activities such as climbing, canoeing and sailing is valuable for everyone, whether dyslexic or not. The focus on physical activity rather than academic learning can be a welcome one. Nevertheless, because dyslexia is often understood as a difficulty with reading and writing, there may be issues that are overlooked by outdoor instructors. For example, many outdoor skills involve sequences, such as the correct sequence of climbing calls, or following an orienteering course. Sequences are problematic in dyslexia, but with careful thought and understanding potential hurdles can easily be avoided.

Instructors in outdoor education need to develop a flexible approach to their teaching and question some long-standing practices. Many people with dyslexia may benefit from seeing the whole picture rather than having it broken down into its constituent parts, for example, and for some a 'building blocks' approach is not helpful. Intuitive understanding of how certain systems work is not unusual, such as how the anchors are constructed in a climbing situation and it is important that instructors are able to recognise this. The same may be true of map reading, where a dyslexic person may be able to interpret the map and follow a route without always being able to describe the various steps involved. For others, however, problems with inverted images or reversed numbers may mean that more imaginative solutions have to be sought.

These points are important when it comes to taking awards and qualifications in outdoor activities. If an instructor or assessor is looking for a set answer to a set question, a dyslexic person may well struggle. If a more flexible approach is adopted however, this need not be the case. Unfortunately many outdoor qualifications include written exam papers or require candidates to give a presentation. These will create additional hurdles and again it should be possible to avoid these by allowing all candidates, whether dyslexic or not, to complete home papers or to put their answers on audio-cassette. What instructors also need to remember is that dyslexic people will often be very well organised in their own workplaces or in their own activities, but may well be working on unfamiliar ground when they attend courses at different centres. This can give an unrealistic picture of someone's organisational skills, which are of course essential in the outdoors.

In teaching outdoor skills a number of strategies can be useful. These approaches benefit all students and often simply represent good teaching practice. The use of colour can be particularly valuable. For example, a widely used knot called a clove hitch can be tied by placing a loop of one colour under a loop of another colour.

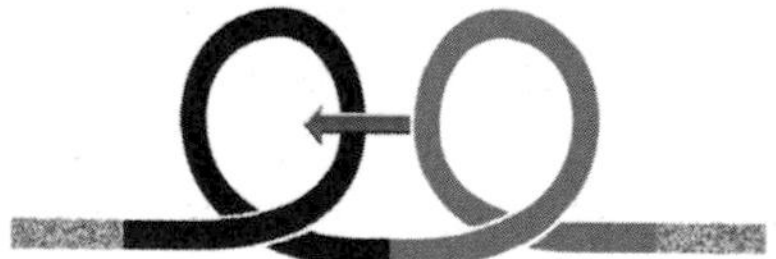

Similarly, problems with direction such as east and west, can be helped by using a red border down the left-hand border of a map, representing west. Concrete images, such as describing a certain type of climbing karabiner as 'pear shaped', may also be helpful. Abstract images, on the other hand are not helpful. So in teaching a technique known as ferry-gliding, comparing the direction of movement of a canoe across a river with the hour hand on a clock is unhelpful. Using a compass for navigating is a skill that will need also need careful teaching, and estimating time may need to be related to a familiar block of time such as a football match, as time is essentially an abstract concept.

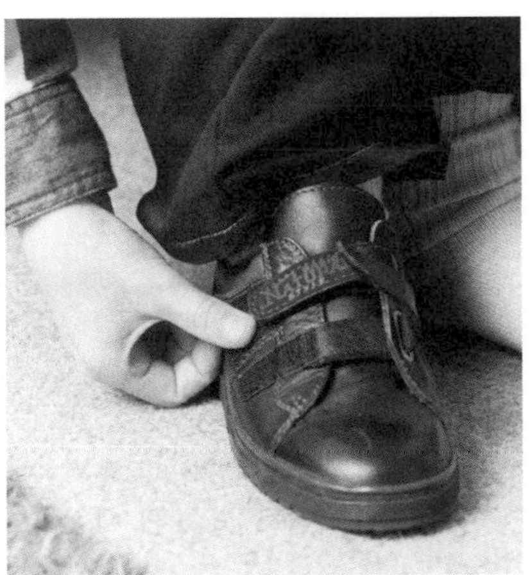

Good practice in other areas is also important. Learning new skills requires practice and repetition in a low stress renvironment. Although the skills applicable to one outdoor sport are often applicable in others (for example many climbing knots are also used in sailing), it is important that they are learnt and practised in one situation before being transferred to another. In acquiring these new skills there are a number of factors than can either help or hinder learning. Again, many of these represent good practice generally, but are essential for someone with dyslexia. In canoeing, for example, it is important that someone is alongside the instructor in their canoe rather than facing them if a new stroke is being demonstrated. Translating a mirror image may be difficult.

The pairing of students in outdoor learning situations needs careful thought. Many people learn most effectively with repeated practice of new skills and it is important that people are not overwhelmed by anecdotes or contradictory information. It is also important to remember that what for many people may simply be background noise, such as at a busy crag, will be a competing stimulus for a dyslexic person and can interfere with learning. Although much outdoor learning takes place away from the classroom, this should not prevent instructors from using straightforward, helpful strategies. It should be possible, for example, to carry laminated cards for use at the crag to explain concepts such as 'fall factors' and instructors should endeavour to ensure that enlarged photocopies of crag diagrams and route descriptions are available, as guidebooks are often difficult to read. If this is not possible, advanced notice of which crags will be used might allow participants to do this themselves.

Finally, it is important to pay attention to the equipment that is given to students who might be attending courses at outdoor centres. For some dyslexic people, clumsiness is a problem and this will be made worse by ill-fitting, borrowed gear. Attention should be paid to the type of compass that is used, as some have very clear dials which are easy to manipulate, whilst others are small and awkward. Joining instructions need to be thorough and include maps *and* written directions, not one or the other, and equipment lists need to be specific, rather than general. Telling students to bring 'equipment for a day on the hill' for example, will not be useful. None of these strategies require specialist knowledge or specialist equipment, but they do require a willingness to be flexible on the part of those teaching outdoor skills.

Dyslexia and Outdoor Learning is an information pack available from Mary Twomey, 26 Hawkshaw Street, Horwich, Lancashire BL6 5NE. The pack costs £3.80 including p&p.

Out of School Clubs

Tracy Pike, Emotional Health Consultant

Out of school hours learning is an activity which young people take part in voluntarily, outside normal school lessons. These activities may take place before commencement of the school day, at lunch times, after school, at weekends or during school holidays. The nature of the programmes is all embracing and covers an exceptionally broad range of activities.

Many children and young people with unidentified learning difficulties such as dyslexia often feel bored, confused and frustrated at school. The ethos of after-school provision is to offer activities that are non-competitive and non-threatening, at a pace appropriate to the individual child.

After-school activities fall into 3 main categories:

Enabling – offering activities to small groups who require additional support with their core skills of literacy, numeracy and ICT.

Extending – offering activities that extend learning experiences such as drama, music, foreign languages, sports and weekend clubs.

Enrichment – offering activities that go beyond the National Curriculum such as fly fishing, samba, golf, circus skills etc.

Many schools acknowledge and celebrate the impact that learning after school hours can have on pupils who might be in danger of being disaffected by what school offers.

Examples

Four schools in England and Wales that have specifically developed out of school provision for dyslexic children have seen the impact that such programmes can have.

Westlands School and Technology College, Torquay offer an after-school club for nine dyslexic boys. Sue Gay is the specialist teacher with responsibility for dyslexia in the school and she set up the club two years ago. Six Year 10 boys and three Year 8 boys have attended the club for two years. The pupils use the 'Touch, Type, Read and Spell' scheme, which has been sponsored by Devon Dyslexia Association. One incentive of attending the club is that the children gain hours towards attendance certificates awarded by the school. Some of the boys have now gained 150 hours. Some of these would otherwise have had high levels of absenteeism in school.

The club called TAG (Thinking Around Group) enjoys the ethos of working as a group, which has greatly improved social skills. They will address good news and bad news which encourages children to talk about good things that have happened that week as a vehicle to improve self esteem. The club has also improved self confidence, by encouraging the boys to talk in front of their peers.

Terrace Road Primary School in Swansea holds a Jumping Jack lunchtime club twice a week. This incorporates an exercise programme that helps children with coordination and those with reading and writing difficulties. The programme is based upon infant movement patterns, acquired during the first 6-9 months of life, which form the foundation for all later voluntary movement. The programme has been successful with dyslexic children.

Combe Pafford School in Torquay, has begun an after-school club in soccer skills for dyslexic children. A teacher at the school found that the repetitive individual drills offered at his Brazilian soccer school, were having a benefit with his students who had dyslexia/dyspraxia. He based his Masters degree dissertation around this and worked with a small group. He noted a tremendous improvement in their writing and coordination. The club now runs weekly.

Melin Primary School in Neath runs a very successful after-school puppet club. Facilitated by the school SENCO, who saw the benefits of repeated reading programmes for dyslexic children, they set up the club up three years ago. Each term the children choose a theme, such as The Simpsons, Beano, Mr Bean etc and write their own script for a play based upon the characters. The characters are depicted in large puppets which are used in the performance. Even the most introverted of children find it easy to perform from behind the puppet. Reading skills have consequently improved once the child's confidence has grown by performing in front of a small group.

The Benefits

There are many benefits for children attending out of school clubs:

- To learn new skills in a relaxed atmosphere.
- To benefit from targeted support.
- To discover new talents and interests.
- To have access to a wider range of facilities and resources.
- To learn about learning in a new way.
- To have somewhere to catch up on work not understood in class.
- To learn at their own speed and in their own way.
- To develop inter-personal and social skills.

- To work in small groups and make new friends.
- To have fun in a safe environment.
- To gain self esteem.
- To achieve more at school.

Throughout the UK there are also many excellent examples of projects that address the emotional health of children, which in turn, of course impacts on self esteem, which is often lacking with dyslexic children. Puppet clubs which explore feelings through the use of vocabulary can be very powerful. Circle time games can have any focus such as conflict and anxiety, change and transition. Role play through drama, addressing the main causes of stress for children such as bullying and peer pressure, can be part of an emotional health programme.

All these activities encourage children to confide their feelings, enabling them to share fears within a secure and non-threatening environment.

Resources

Further resource materials for emotional health incentive plus suppliers www.incentiveplus.co.uk Tel 01908 526120

Organisation support for Out Of School Hours Learning contact ContinYou. www.continyou.org.uk.
Tel 020 8709 9900

Wave 3 Interventions

Jean Gross, Senior Director (Achievement and Inclusion), Primary National Strategy

The Primary National Strategy was launched in May 2003, to sustain and extend the work of the National Literacy and Numeracy Strategies. Its work is described in the policy document *Excellence and Enjoyment* – a vision for primary education setting out every child's right to a broad and rich curriculum with high standards in literacy and numeracy at its core.

Excellence and Enjoyment flagged up the concern the government has for children who experience significant difficulties in literacy, mathematics or both, and outlines plans to support schools in improving the effectiveness of their provision for these children.

The model used is one of 'Waves' of support

- **Wave 1** – The effective inclusion of all children in a daily and high quality literacy hour and daily mathematics lesson.
- **Wave 2** – Additional small-group intervention for children who can be expected to catch up with others of the same age as a result of the intervention.

- **Wave 3** – Specific targeted approaches for children identified as having persisting literacy or mathematics difficulties requiring SEN intervention.

Wave 1

The Primary National Strategy has provided guidance to schools on what effective everyday teaching of the literacy hour and daily mathematics lesson should look like for dyslexic children. The guidance suggests some simple strategies such as making sure dyslexic children have 'study buddies' whose skills complement their own; for example, a child who has good ideas for writing (composition) but difficulty in spelling and handwriting (transcription) is paired for recording tasks with a child who is good at transcription but not composition, or a child who is good with numbers and the number system is paired with a child who finds this difficult, but is good at work on shape and space.

More detailed guidance is in preparation, being written for the Strategy by Lindsay Peer, a dyslexia consultant, together with LEA literacy and numeracy consultants. This will take the form of a CD-ROM of training materials a school could use with all staff to help them gain a greater understanding of how to make their classrooms more dyslexia-friendly.

Wave 2 Interventions

Many dyslexic children take part in work in small groups, within the literacy hour or additional to it, supported by a trained teaching assistant on programmes like Early Literacy Support (ELS), which is aimed at helping children in Year 1 (around the age of 6) who are beginning to fall behind in their reading, spelling and writing to catch up with their peers – long before they start to feel discouraged and frustrated. Later on, they might have extra help with mathematics though a 'Springboard' programme, working again in a group with a teaching assistant, or in Year 5 through a programme called Further Literacy Support which is targeted particularly at children who are finding it hard to motivate themselves and who need help with their writing. All these programmes aim to give a quick boost to learning and are for children who can, given this kind of boost, achieve at the nationally expected level for their age.

Wave 3 Interventions

Whilst the right kind of classroom teaching and, in some cases, Wave 2 catch-up programmes are important to dyslexic children, many will have needs that require more substantial and individualised additional help.

At the moment, schools and other agencies providing support for children with literacy difficulties make use of a wide range of different teaching interventions. The schemes and programmes in use vary widely in the extent to which they have been evaluated and the evidence-base for their effectiveness.

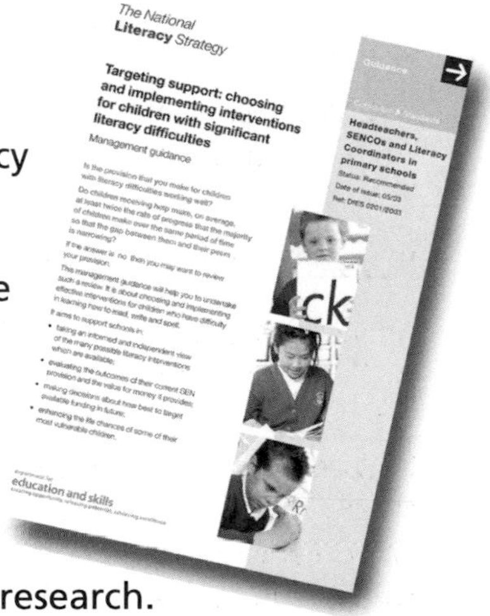

Because of this, the government commissioned some research on the impact of the various schemes and programmes for children with literacy difficulties, including many that are used with dyslexic children, to see which ones do appear to 'work'. The research, by Professor Greg Brooks, looked at forty schemes and programmes, and is well worth reading. A government leaflet for all primary schools was subsequently published, summarising the evidence from the research. The leaflet gives schools practical guidance on how to check that their own Wave 3 provision matches up to the best of what is now available.

Local education authorities (LEAs) have been asked to play an active role in drawing this guidance to schools' attention. They have been asked to encourage their primary schools to track very carefully the progress of children who experience literacy difficulties, and plan effective additional provision for children where necessary. Many LEAs have organised conferences and workshops for headteachers and school special needs coordinators, at which they can look at specific programmes and plan which are right for their children.

Some LEAs are identifying schools with really good practice in this area to act as leaders – places where other schools can visit and from which they can get advice.

Wave 3 and mathematics

Difficulties in aspects of mathematics are often a feature of dyslexia, but can sometimes get missed when a school is planning support. Schools also have fewer schemes and programmes to draw on in mathematics than they do in literacy. Those that exist have been reviewed in another research report commissioned by the DfES, *What works for children with mathematical difficulties*.

Key findings from this research were that:

- difficulties in mathematics are common , and as common in girls as in boys (unlike literacy difficulties, which are very much more common in boys);
- they do not reflect a lack of ability or effort and are not the fault of children or their parents;
- they represent one end of a continuum rather than a discrete 'disorder';
- they can be addressed through appropriate intervention;
- intervention should be as early as possible; and

- many children with dyslexic difficulties also experience difficulties in mathematics.

Dr Anne Dowker, who wrote the report, also concluded that there is no one single pattern of mathematical difficulties; every child is different. Nevertheless, difficulties in memory for number facts and in solving multi-step 'word' problems are common features.

Just as there is no single pattern of difficulties, so there is no single teaching approach or programme that will be right for every child. Instead, intervention by a teacher or teaching assistant should focus on the particular components of numeracy with which each individual child is struggling.

The Primary National Strategy is using these principles to design and try out teaching activities that can be used to give extra help, on a 'little and often' basis, for children aged seven to eleven. This Wave 3 package will be available to all schools from spring 2005.

Parents and the 3 Waves of Intervention

Finally, what should all this mean for parents in terms of what they should expect from their child's school?

First, the school should increasingly be able to describe the provision it makes at each of the three waves, including effective strategies for teaching phonics, spelling and basic number skills to all children at Wave 1, appropriate use of small-group programmes at Wave 2, and carefully planned provision at Wave 3.

Secondly, you should be able to discuss with the school the extent to which your child's classroom is 'dyslexia-friendly' and what strategies your child finds particularly helpful.

Don't be surprised, however, if all this is not quite in place yet! All parents know that schools are incredibly busy places these days, and that teachers can at times feel overwhelmed by the volume of materials and guidance available to them. You can help by showing that you understand these pressures, and working together with the school to pick out those elements that are likely to be helpful to you both in your joint task of securing the best possible learning opportunities for your child.

Further Reading

What works for children with literacy difficulties (DfES Research Report 380) and *What works for children with mathematical difficulties* (DfES Research Report 554) are available from DfES Publications, tel: 0845 60 222 60 and cost £4.95. They are also available on the DfES research website www.dfes.gov.uk/research.

The guidance on what effective everyday teaching of the literacy hour and daily mathematics lesson should look like for dyslexic children can be found in the publication *Including all children in the literacy hour and daily mathematics lesson* (DfES 0465/2002). This can be ordered by schools only from DfES publications, but is available on the DfES standards website: www.standards.dfes.gov.uk/primary. Also on the inclusion section of this website is *Guidance to support pupils with specific needs in the daily mathematics lesson* (DfES 0545/2001), the leaflet *Targeting support: choosing and implementing interventions for children with significant literacy difficulties* (DfES 0201/2003) as well as answers to Frequently Asked Questions about dyslexia, dyscalculia and mathematics.

Language, Phonology and Beginning to Read

Dr Valerie Muter, Centre for Reading & Language, University of York

When children start school, they face one of the biggest challenges in their whole lifetime of learning – that of learning to read. For some children, this is an easy and rewarding experience; for others, it is difficult and frustrating. Making a good early start in learning to read generates enormous benefits for the individual child. Long term research studies have shown that children who make sound early progress in reading, not only read more books but also understand far better what they read, even at age 16, than those children who get off to a slow start.

There has been an enormous amount of research over the past twenty years that looks at how young normally developing children acquire reading skills. What is understood about early reading processes (and how they can go wrong) stems largely from research into "predictors" of reading ability. Predictors are skills or abilities that have been demonstrated to contribute to reading development, and which are definable, measurable and potentially modifiable through teaching. For very young children, these predictors indicate what underlying cognitive skills or abilities they need to have in place to enable them to begin to learn to read. In general, it is language-based abilities that form the foundation on which the child's reading skill is built. It is not a coincidence that children begin to read after they have developed spoken language abilities sufficient to underpin their emerging knowledge of the printed word.

Predictors of Early Reading Ability

The most extensively studied of the predictors of reading ability is that of *phonological awareness*. This refers to children's sensitivity to the speech sound structure of words. We can demonstrate, and in fact measure, phonological awareness in children from 4–7 years by asking them to:

- produce words that rhyme with each other (cat, mat, fat);
- blend sounds together to make words (c-a-t join together to make /cat/);
- identify or supply the final sound of a word ("t" in /cat/); and
- manipulate sounds in words by, for instance, deleting them (/cat/ without the "c" says /at/).

Young children's ability to carry out tasks like these is a powerful predictor of their later reading ability.

Phonological awareness is a skill that develops steadily during the pre-school years. Children's understanding of the sound structure of words proceeds from initially large segments (like syllables) to increasingly smaller segments (eventually, phonemes). This awareness of segmental size is thought to be driven by earlier vocabulary growth, specifically a spurt that takes place between 18 and 30 months of age. The child's first 50 words or so are acquired slowly, and one at a time, but from about 18 months of age, there is a large and sudden increase in the number of words they can produce and comprehend. As the growing number of words overlap in their sound-based properties, there is considerable pressure to develop fine-grained or segmental representations of these in the child's memory store. It seems that vocabulary growth contributes to the early stages of phonological awareness development, but it does not play a continuing role. It would appear that the further growth of increasingly refined phonological awareness (e.g. awareness of phonemes) simply evolves from earlier established phonological skills (like awareness of syllables).

Another important predictor of early reading success is children's ease of acquiring *letter knowledge*. Children who rapidly acquire knowledge of basic sound-to-letter relationships make far faster progress in learning to read than children who are slow to learn their letters.

Phonological awareness and letter knowledge influence early reading development partly as separate skills, but also in interaction with one another. In other words, the child's improving speech sound sensitivity "links or merges" with their developing letter knowledge to fuel progress in reading. When children make this important "linkage", they become *alphabetic readers.* They begin to understand that letters systematically represent the sounds of their language. Once they can do this, they start to develop "decoding" (or sounding out) strategies which set them up for becoming independent readers. Indeed, the child's acquisition of this *alphabetic principle* forms the foundation for the rapid expansion of their reading vocabulary during their first two years at school.

The contribution of phonological awareness, vocabulary and letter knowledge to early reading skill (from pre-school through nursery to reception) is shown in the following diagram:

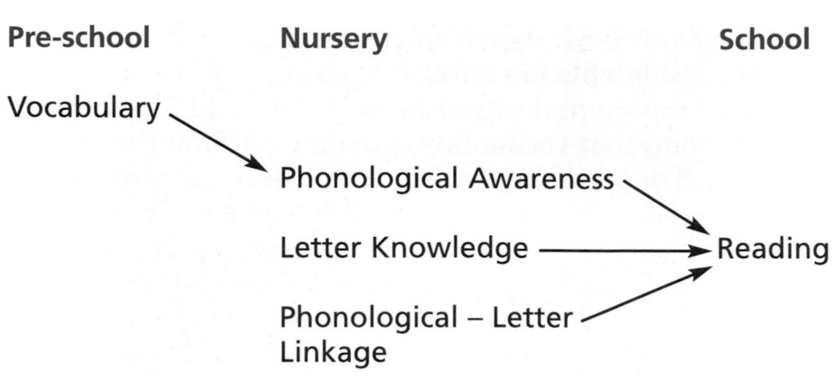

Dyslexic children have significant difficulty in developing phonological skills and in acquiring alphabet letter knowledge. Consequently, these important pathways to early reading progress are severely compromised in these children. They fail to acquire the alphabetic principle and so find it hard to make use of decoding strategies that are so critical for the development of independent reading.

How Can We Use Predictor Skills to Help Children Read?

There are a number of practical applications of the research into predictors of early reading skill.

- First, parents at home can contribute a lot to getting their children off to a good start in literacy by *reading story books* to them (which helps develop and expand their spoken vocabulary knowledge), and by working through alphabet books with them (to increase their letter awareness and knowledge).
- Predictor measures can be used as assessment tools for *screening* – that is, to identify which young children (as young as 5 years, in fact) will find reading easy and which will find it difficult; screening instruments such as the Phonological Abilities Test (PAT) consist of a series of simple phonological games that test children's ability to

rhyme, segment and delete sounds within words, as well as demonstrate their knowledge of the alphabet.

- Once we know which children are "at risk" of reading failure, we can "target" them in some way. For instance, by monitoring their future progress, or more pro-actively, training up those predictor skills with which they are experiencing difficulty, we can teach 4–5 year old children to identify or delete sounds in words. Playing sound blending or rhyming games may help to *prevent* them developing reading problems.

- Predictor measures have been used to develop *diagnostic instruments* for assessing children with reading difficulties, including dyslexic children (for instance, the PAT and the Phonological Assessment Battery, PhAB, here in the UK, and the Comprehensive Test of Phonological Processing, CTOPP, in the US).
- Finally, phonological awareness training has increasingly been incorporated into *classroom teaching* programmes and specialist reading schemes; intervention studies have shown that explicit instruction in phonological awareness (especially when it is directly linked to learning about letters and printed words) can accelerate children's progress in learning to read.

In understanding the components of early reading development, we now have the tools to help children to learn to read more easily and to even prevent reading failure. The impact of this knowledge on children's future educational success and their long-term behavioural adjustment cannot be underestimated.

References

The Phonological Abilities Test by V. Muter, C. Hulme and M. Snowling
Available through the Psychological Corporation UK.

The Phonological Assessment Battery (PhAB) by N. Frederickson, U. Frith and R. Reason.
Available through NFER-Nelson.

The Comprehensive Test of Phonological Processing (CTOPP) by R. Wagner, J. Torgesen and C. Rashotte.
Available through Pro-Ed (in the US).

Speech and Language – A Brilliant Self-Marketing Tool

Diana Crewdson, Speech and Language Therapist

We may be enchanted, moved, amused and entertained by Susan Hampshire, Whoopie Goldberg, Eddie Izzard, Nicholas Parsons, Art Malik, Tom Cruise, Anthea Turner, Toyah Wilcox, Anthony Hopkins, Jeremy Irons, Bob Hoskins, Sarah Brightman, Ruth Madoc... and more. There are politicians and celebrity chefs in our 'Dyslexic Hall of Fame' too. They have all used their skill and style in spoken language to build successful careers. Spoken language is their most important 'Self-marketing' tool.

Whilst dyslexic learners have shown that they benefit from structured support for reading, writing, spelling and study skills, it is equally important to develop their skills and confidence in spoken language. For most of us spoken communication will be our 'front line' in showing our interests, enthusiasms and abilities to friends, colleagues, teachers, employers or clients.

Dyslexia is often associated with some delay in early speech and language development when compared with other skills. Many dyslexic people continue to be frustrated by needing time to remember specific words or explain things in a clear sequence. For some this can be an irritating contrast to their speed in picturing whole events or considering solutions to problems.

A central feature of dyslexia is difficulty with phonological processing. This describes noticing the detail and sequence of sounds in words and recreating and varying those sequences. Fragile phonological skills can be associated with varying degrees of inefficiency in other areas of spoken language:

- Listening carefully.
- Noticing the difference between similar speech sounds and their positions in words.
- Pronouncing all the speech sounds clearly and consistently.
- Understanding the meaning of words, parts of speech and sentences.
- Finding the right words to describe, ask or explain.
- Understanding and using increasingly complex sentences.
- Understanding and using the subtle extra clues to meaning evident in changes of intonation and volume.
- Using different styles for different people and situations.
- Being able to follow and explain a sequence of events.

Some children's speech or language difficulties will be evident in the early years. They may be helped by advice or support from a speech and language therapist or specialist teacher. For most dyslexic people any lingering speech and language difficulties are subtle and not noticed in informal conversation. They have a greater effect when language is written down, because then the words and their order have to be specific and correct.

As with literacy, spoken language can be encouraged from the 'bottom up' and the 'top down'.

'Bottom up' activities develop the skills that underpin good communication. These might include:

DfES Approved. ISA. CReSTeD 'SP'
DfES 'Highly Effective School' DfES 'Beacon School'
ISA 'Award for Excellence' 'National Training Award'
Sportsmark Award 'with distinction'

Mark College has an international reputation for its educational work with dyslexics. It's goal is straightforward, to provide a top class education for its pupils. To help achieve this goal, it has superb facilities and a staff whose skill and experience have taken our pupils' GCSE results to levels described as 'outstanding' by Ofsted. What Mark College does is to remove the barriers to learning so that its pupils experience a 'normal' education.

Mark College is also recognised for its care. It's work with pupils' self-esteem and self-confidence was the subject of a University study. The conclusions from this independent study have been presented at three international conferences. We are very proud of the findings from this research.

Mark College, Mark, Highbridge, Somerset TA9 4NP
ph 01278 641 632 fax 01278 641 426
www.markcollege.somerset.sch.uk post@markcollege.somerset.sch.uk

- **Listening carefully.** Regularly listening to appropriate music can help to 'wake up' awareness of detail. It can be a useful starting point, particularly for those who have a history of early intermittent hearing loss. Mozart works well, but a specific programme of listening can provide the structure and the correct quality and variety of sound to get the maximum benefit.
- Listening to the best possible audio-recording of **one's own voice** and using this as a basis for comprehension and dictation activities encourages attention and memory for detail. The principles of the ARROW© system work well. Listening to our own voice also encourages inner language to support memory, planning and learning.
- **Visualising what we hear** helps with understanding, word finding, and staying on the topic. Visualising can be encouraged by talking together about how we remember or imagine things.
- **Practice in multi-tasking.** Being able to use language at the same time as looking and doing is important for many activities in school and life. These include deciding what it is most important to attend to, taking in instructions whilst working and taking notes. Combine an activity such as passing an object from hand to hand or some of the bilateral integration exercises from Brain Gym© with:
  - reciting tables or the alphabet;
  - generating words in a category such as colours, animals, parts of the flower or elements and compounds; and
  - answering short questions – good for review and revision.

'Top down' activities give guided practice in using speech and language well. These might include:

- **Daily time to talk.** If a child has experienced muddled sound input because of fluctuating hearing problems, it can have a significant impact on their awareness of sounds in words. They may also have missed much of the incidental language noticed by those who hear easily and consistently. It is particularly important for these children to have daily calm talk time with one adult in a quiet room so that they can notice the detail in slow clear speech. Teenagers also need to practise conversational skills, even though they don't always appreciate that the adults in their lives might prefer to do this at a reasonable time of day!

- **Listening for key words** is a simple and effective way of supporting attention to spoken input in the classroom. If the teacher puts two useful words on the board at the start of the lesson, pupils can write them in the back of their exercise book and tick beneath each word whenever they hear it. The act of purposeful listening helps pupils to get back into the topic if their mind has wandered. I have heard that the ex-queen of the Netherlands used a similar strategy. She reported that, as Queen, she had to listen to many long speeches, and there is nothing more boring than NOT listening to a long speech!
- **Asking effective questions and asking for more information.** Good questions and requests please the listener by letting them know that we are interested. Unfortunately, if we ask or request at the wrong time or in the wrong way, it can appear cheeky or be ignored. Parents can help by modelling and planning good questions and giving explicit feedback e.g. 'That was a good question because . . . .'. Teachers can help by creating an atmosphere where it's good to question, challenge or admit uncertainty – as long as it is done politely.
- **Everyone should know that:**
  - a message cannot always be understood;
  - it is OK not to understand and good to ask;
  - it may be the speaker's fault because they did not speak clearly or give enough information – we all do this sometimes; and

- it may be the listener's fault because they forgot or stopped listening – we all do this sometimes too.

- **Everyone should be able to:**
  - acknowledge when they haven't understood;
  - be specific about what they have not understood;
  - be able to say why they have not understood; and
  - ask and explain politely.

In the early years, progress in speech and spoken language precedes each stage of literacy development and it is exciting that this is receiving greater recognition through the Primary National Strategy's first main publication for teachers focusing on speaking and listening.

For many adults, spoken language increasingly supersedes reading and writing. We have mobile phones, video-conferencing and the mobility to rely on more inter-personal contact. For all of us, time given to teaching and practising talking is very well spent.

References

Visualising and Verbalising for Language Comprehension and Thinking. Bell, N from Winslow Tel: 0800 243755

Speaking, Listening, Learning: working with children in Key Stage 1 and 2. Primary National Strategy (2003) DfES Publications 0623 – 8 2003 G

ARROW information from: ARROW Tuition Ltd
Tel/ Fax: 01278 441249 www.self-voice.co.uk

For more information on Arrow – see page 304

Brain Gym © books and information from: Educational Kinesiology (UK) Tel: 020 8202 3141 Fax: 020 8202 3890

Listening and Sound Therapy information from:
www.johansensoundtherapy.com and
www.advancedbrain.com

Hannah Cox

16 year old Hannah Cox is celebrating her recent successful GCSE results. Unlike other young students, Hannah's celebrations are particularly significant. Until she was prescribed with CromaGen™ spectacle lenses, Hannah may have had little hope of passing her exams.

Hannah was diagnosed with dyslexia 2 years ago, having silently suffered throughout her education, struggling with spelling, slow and poor reading and requiring extra time for sitting exam papers.

Since wearing her CromaGen™ lenses, Hannah reports "almost immediately the text stays on the page, my reading and writing significantly improved and I could absorb information much easier". This assistance helped Hannah to sit her exams as a confident, articulate student and now her recent exam results have enabled her to plan her A Levels and future university education.

Multiple Intelligences and Dyslexia

Ann Cooke, Dyslexia Unit, University of Wales Bangor

Intelligence, and intelligent, are words we use frequently when we talk about mental capability, thinking and reasoning, and how we construct new ideas, or solve problems by using our knowledge and experience. But *can* there be more than one kind of intelligence?
The Concise Oxford Dictionary specifies that, when used of machines or computer systems, 'intelligent' means 'able to respond and adapt', and that applies to humans too. 'Intelligence' is what enables you to do well in school, and to pass exams. It's certainly not 'instinct' – that's how animals think – and more than plain 'common sense', which is what helps us to get by in ordinary life.

But there have been challenges to the concept of 'intelligence', particularly to the idea that it can be measured, and even more to the notion of Intelligence Quotient, or IQ. People use this term to quantify 'reasoning ability', especially of children and students, and to make decisions about resources, or who gets a place in a 'good' school.

Specifically, IQ is criticised because the tests by which it is calculated can give only a limited picture of an individual's capabilities. There is no scope for a creative approach, or to count points for success in activities that are not in the test. Teachers hear parents say that their child can't get going in reading and can't learn spellings, yet the child seems bright and intelligent and is certainly not stupid. Teachers note the same kind of puzzle – the child who can give an oral answer but can't write it down. What are they saying?

I think they are saying that reading and spelling ability is not the only way to 'size up' a child; that there are other aptitudes, other ways of doing things that get results. The trouble is, if you can't read, and even more, if you can't write efficiently (because that is what earns the marks) you will have to struggle for success and good results in tests and exams. Many teachers, and other students, will assume you are 'stupid' and you may even come to believe them.

This is where 'multiple intelligences' comes in. In his book *Frames of Mind*, Professor Howard Gardner argues that there is more than one way for human beings to be 'intelligent'. Because the capacity for language based on speech is part of our human make up, built into our brains over millions of years, we have come to assume that 'intelligence' – the ability to think and reason – requires words. In discussing Linguistic Intelligence Gardner points out that the versatility and variety of human language enables it to serve many purposes: it can be a medium for creative expression, a tool for instruction, for giving information and for all kinds of communication. We can speak it, using our auditory-oral senses, or write it, when it becomes a visual and kinaesthetic medium, except for the non-sighted, who read kinaesthetically through Braille. It is truly multisensory.

But word-language is only one of several systems by which we can operate. Creative and artistic activity is beyond 'thought'. A composer does not work by verbal reasoning, and neither does the performer; they work through experimenting with sounds, and listening – often in their heads. Words are secondary tools in their art; they do not work through writing essays! But music uses symbols, and so does mathematics, for communication and to process information, just as written language does and we often refer to musical, or mathematical 'languages'. In that way they are similar to written language.

We all function in different ways. Let's go back to the individual who finds reading difficult, but is not 'stupid'. She, or he, may seem to have an automatic understanding of how things work – computer, video, different kinds of machinery. These people may work through watching and doing, and they often have a 'feel' for how to get results. Others, architects and engineers, for instance, may picture, or construct, and manipulate their 'ideas', in their head, bypassing word-based language. A sculptor and painter will experiment and look at their work, feel how the tool shapes the material, or the way the paint flows onto the canvas. If they are not good readers or writers, are they therefore unintelligent? Gardner argues that such spatial and bodily kinaesthetic ways of working are also examples of 'intelligence.' He includes dancers, actors, sportsmen and sportswomen in this group. Their responses and their performance are in-built – though they also put in long hours of practice and training. They do not have time to 'think' when they are in action.

Mathematical ability is an obvious member of the 'multiple intelligence' group. (Gardner calls it Logical-Mathematical Intelligence.) Here we can find many examples of extremes, such as the person who can calculate at great speed, processing information in a way that would be impossible for most of us. (Try doing a long multiplication sum in your head!) How do they work? By specialised ways of 'thinking' – including using patterns and numerical relationships. Some students have difficulty remembering and saying times-tables (which relies on verbal memory) but they may be good at geometry, for which they draw on understanding of spatial relationships.

In any individual, the mix of 'intelligences' will be different; in some people, particular aspects may be highly developed, while others inadequate or even absent. Christopher, in *The Curious Incident of the Dog in the Nighttime*, is an example. He has Asperger's Syndrome and excels at mathematics and science, but he does not understand people.

Gardner includes 'Personal Intelligences' in his list. These are shown by people who have exceptional understanding of how to interact with others, to empathise, or sense others' needs. They might be carers, or nurses, or just 'good with' old people or little children; they seem to work by intuition. (David Goleman takes this further and talks about 'Emotional Intelligence')

By now, readers will have spotted that many dyslexic individuals fit into this picture. Here, the theory of multiple intelligences seems to interrelate with ideas about right and left brain hemisphere preference. Dyslexic people often seem to work better with 'right-hemisphere' activity where a global, or whole view, approach can be taken; working with details in a sequential way – a 'left-hemisphere' activity – is more difficult for them. So problems arise with learning and using systems which operate through symbols – languages, mathematics and music do; and examinations which rely on performance in these domains give extra trouble. But these ideas should not be over-pressed. Gardner himself points out that neurological organisation is highly complex and still little understood. In his book, *In the Mind's Eye*, Thomas West emphasises that you can be 'intelligent' without having formal academic abilities. He cites many historical examples of people who might now be called dyslexic:

- Michael Faraday, the 18th century genius of chemistry.
- The sculptor Rodin, who had difficulty learning to read.
- Winston Churchill, who was not clever at school – but became first a journalist, then a great politician, a historian and a writer, as well as a talented painter. He also enjoyed bricklaying!

Gardner's arguments are persuasive – and unemotional. Tom West's are persuasive and passionate in his promotion of the 'mind's eye' and of those who work in non-linguistic ways. Their skills are needed, he argues, for the development of new and essential technology.

Reading and writing are latecomers into the frame of ways of thinking. The duty of schools to teach everyone to read and write (and the expectation that everyone could learn literacy skills) dates, in Britain, from 1870. But there are other – older – ways of learning and functioning. Multisensory approaches have a long-established place in teaching systems for dyslexic learners; that should mean, to some extent, that each individual's preferred style of learning should be met. But we could be doing more. If we accept Gardner's theory of Multiple Intelligences, and keep it in mind in our teaching, we may help to show that non-linguistic ways of working are not only valuable, but necessary.

For teachers, exam-setters, parents, and dyslexic learners themselves, the implications could be huge.

References

Howard Gardner. "Frames of Mind: The Theory of Multiple Intelligences" 2nd edition (1993) London, Fontana.

Daniel Goleman. "Emotional Intelligence" (1996) Bloomsbury, London.

Mark Haddon. "The Curious Incident of the Dog in the Nighttime" (2003) Vintage, London.

Thomas G West "In the Mind's Eye" (1997) Prometheus Books, New York.

Writing the Facts

David Wray, University of Warwick, and
Maureen Lewis, National Primary Strategy

Introduction

One of the most interesting features of recent initiatives in literacy teaching is the issue of genre, or text type. The framework of teaching objectives for the National Literacy Strategy is organised around text type, focusing on a different type in each school term.

Many teachers would claim they have always provided such variety in terms of fiction texts. Certainly, one of the major features of modern approaches to teaching reading is the emphasis upon broadening children's literacy experiences to include fables, myths and legends, adventure stories, poetry etc. Few children emerge nowadays from primary schools with experiences limited to traditional reading scheme 'stories'.

Yet there remain some problems with non-fiction texts. The writing of factual texts seems particularly problematic.

The Problems of Factual Writing

Writing causes several problems for those not skilled at it. We have identified four major problem areas.

a) The blank page

Most writers will agree that the hardest part of writing is the first line or two. Getting started can be so difficult, even for experienced writers, that they invent 'delaying tactics' (sharpening pencils, making coffee) to put off the awful moment. A blank page can be daunting and for many inexperienced writers it can result in abandonment of the writing. We have explored whether providing learner writers with pages already containing some text might ease the writing.

b) Talking and writing

When talking to another, we receive constant support for our language. Talking is usually a dialogue, that is, one person says something, and this prompts the other person to reply, which in turn prompts the first person, and so on. Talkers receive continual prompts for their language.

Writers, on the contrary, get no such prompts. They are by themselves, forced to produce language without support from another. Of course, in a classroom, there is potential support, from a teacher who may be at a child's shoulder saying such things as:

> *"That's an interesting idea. Tell us more about that."*
> *"You've made a good point. Can you tell us why you think that?"*

It is difficult, however, in a classroom with up to 35 child writers, for a teacher to be able to provide such support for the whole class. We needed ways of providing support for writers that did not require the physical presence of the teacher.

c) The 'and then' syndrome

Inexperienced writers tend to have a limited range of ways of joining together ideas in writing. Most primary teachers will recognise this by the prevalence of 'and then' in their children's writing, as if this were the only way of linking ideas in writing. We were interested in strategies for helping young writers to broaden the range of connectives they could use.

d) The structure of non-fiction texts

Many children lack experience of the different types of non-fiction texts and their organisational structures. They need help in distinguishing between these in terms of vocabulary, connectives and structure. A concept which can help here is that of text genre.

According to genre theory, pieces of writing which share a common purpose will tend to share a common structure. One language purpose might be to provide instructions for someone to do a task, e.g. a recipe. Such instructions will tend to follow a pattern:

1 A statement of the goal. (e.g. How to make a chocolate cake.)

2 A list of materials necessary. (e.g. You will need ....)

3 A series of steps to follow. (e.g. First you ...., Then ....)

Language patterns such as this become so routine that we are barely aware of them, yet clearly they have to be learnt. Many children will find such structures difficult because they do not have the right expectations about texts. It is common, for example, for children to write instructions in the form of a narrative; "I got some sugar and put it in a bowl. Then I ...." Teachers need to teach children to use a range of language structures for appropriate purposes.

In order to do this, teachers need to be aware of the range of factual text genres. We have suggested that there are six basic factual genres: Recount, Report, Discussion, Persuasion, Explanation, Instructions (Wray & Lewis, 1997). Research suggests that primary children get lots of experience of writing recounts but rarely the other genres. This imbalance is important because in later life these other genres are very heavily used and are crucial to success.

Supporting Writing

As a way of supporting children's writing in a range of genres, we have found writing frames useful. A frame provides a skeleton structural outline for a piece of writing around which children have to structure their own ideas. There are many possible frames for each genre but one example for Discussion genre is given in Figure 1.

There is a lot of discussion about whether

....

The people who agree with this idea, such as.............., claim that ....

They also argue that..

However, there are also strong arguments against this point of view. .... believe that

....

Furthermore, ...

After looking at the different points of view and the evidence for them I think .... because ....

Figure 1: A discussion writing frame

Notice how writing with the frame overcomes the four writing problems.

a) It no longer presents writers with a blank page. There is comfort in the fact that there is already some writing here. This alone can encourage weaker writers to write at greater length.

b) The frame provides a series of prompts to writing, each prompt following a written contribution from the child. Using the frame is rather like having a dialogue with the page.

c) The frame deliberately includes connectives beyond the simple 'and then'. We have found that extended use of frames like this can result in children spontaneously using these more elaborate connectives in other writing.

d) The frame is designed around the typical structure of discussion genre. It thus gives children access to this structure and implicitly teaches how to write it.

Using this discussion frame helped ten-year-old Kerry write a discussion about boxing (Figure 2). The frame encouraged her to structure the discussion to look at both sides of the argument.

It is clear from our work that use of frames like these has improved the factual writing of children, particularly those with difficulties. Many children have been able to use the frames and then go beyond them to produce writing showing their understanding about writing structures. We see this 'moving beyond writing frames' as particularly important.

Moving Beyond Writing Frames

Writing frames have a clear appeal in that they can quickly transform children's' non-fiction writing into appropriately structured and worded pieces. There is, however, a danger if they are not used carefully that formulaic writing can result. Frames can be over-used.

It should be obvious that children need to use the frames less and less as their knowledge of a particular form increases. At this later stage, when children begin to show

Boxing

Kerry Williams

There is a lot of discussion about whether boxing should be banned. The people who agree with this idea, such as Sarah, claim that if they do carry on boxing they should wear something to protect their heads. They also argue that people who do boxing could have brain damage and get seriously hurt. A further point they make is that most of the people that have died did have families.

However, there are also strong arguments against this point of view. Another group of people believe that boxing should not be banned. They say that why did they invent it if it is a dangerous sport. They say that boxing is a good sport, people enjoy it. A furthermore reason is if they ban boxing it will ruin people's careers.

After looking at the different points of view and the evidence for them I think boxing should be banned because five hundred people have died in boxing since 1884.

Figure 2: A discussion written using a writing frame

evidence of independent usage, the teacher may only need to have master copies of the frames available as help cards for use when children need them.

Also, as children become familiar with the frame structures, there are a number of alternative supports, such as sheets containing lists of possible ways of connecting ideas together. A number of these will be found in Lewis & Wray (1998).

Conclusion

It is important that frames are not seen simply as worksheets. They are only useful when there is a clear purpose for a particular piece of writing. We would also recommend that children need a great deal of experience of other ways of producing writing at the same time as using the frames. Experience has shown, however, that using frames such as these can improve children's writing in a range of genres. They are particularly beneficial for children who find writing difficult.

References

Wray, D. & Lewis, M. (1997) *Extending Literacy,* London: Routledge

Lewis, M. & Wray, D. (1998) *Writing across the Curriculum,* Reading: University of Reading Reading and Language Information Centre.

Address for correspondence

Professor David Wray
Institute of Education
Coventry
CV1 4AL
Tel: 024 7652 2057
Email: d.j.wray@warwick.ac.uk

Assessing the Self Concept and Self Esteem of Children and Adults with Dyslexia

Bob Burden PhD, Professor of Applied Educational Psychology, University of Exeter

There has long been considerable research evidence to show the importance of the connection between how people feel about themselves and their achievements at school or in their adult life. More than twenty years ago Burns (1982) provided a comprehensive review of the self concept in education in which he was able to cite dozens of studies emphasising this relationship. Although questions remain as the causative nature of this relationship (do you do well because you feel good about yourself or do you feel good about yourself because you are doing well?), there is no doubt that, if we add the results of self concept measures to intelligence test scores we can significantly improve our predictions of academic success.

Surprisingly few studies have been carried out into how dyslexic children and adults think and feel about themselves (see Humphrey & Mullins, 2002; Burden & Burdett, 2004a)

partly because of the dearth of appropriate assessment techniques and the complex way in which self concepts develop. Studies in the United States with children with learning disabilities, however have shown that, compared with good readers of comparable age, sex and intelligence, underachieving readers tend to display feelings of discouragement, inadequacy, anxiety and frustration. These feelings can themselves become part of a self fulfilling prophesy leading to further underachievement. It therefore becomes important to break into this downward cycle, not only by means of effective remedial methods, but also by building up underachievers' feelings of confidence and capability to succeed.

There are three important stages in this process, the first of which is an accurate assessment of how the underachieving dyslexic students feel about themselves as learners. This should be followed by steps to improve the student's (or individual adult's) academic self concept and self esteem.

The results of this should be evaluated by methods which include both self concept/self esteem measures as well as indicators of goal achievements or improved attainments.

Self Concept

Although the terms "self concept" and "self esteem" are often used interchangeably, they actually have very different meanings. The term self concept is usually used to refer to a combination of the whole range of ways in which we make sense of ourselves and our lives. Thus we may have rather different views of ourselves as parents, lovers, academics, successful business persons, singers etc. All of which together make up our general self concept. Measurement scales that have been developed to tap into people's self concepts have usually identified five or six key areas and produced a number of items relating to these areas. The responses of all of these are then added together to give a General Self Concept score or are presented as a profile of different subscale scores. The most well known and widely used scales of this kind are those constructed by Harter and Marsh (see Byrne, 1996). The advantages of such scales are that they are well standardised (but not usually in the UK) and widely used with strong statistical evidence of validity and reliability. Their potential weaknesses are that they tend to be long and time consuming to administer, score and interpret, particularly when administered to those with literacy difficulties, and may only contain relatively few items devoted to a person's learning self concept.

An alternative approach to self concept measurements is to focus on one specific sub area such as body image, sporting ability, general academic ability or, even more specifically, reading or mathematical ability. This approach has the advantage of producing briefer and more focused scales which tend to be easier to administer and score. However, it lays no claim to providing information about a respondent's more general self concept or any other aspect of it.

One scale of this nature which is becoming increasingly widely used by teachers and psychologists is the "Myself-as-a-Learner Scale (MALS). This was specifically constructed to provide a relatively brief, valid and reliable measure of the sense that people make of their learning capabilities (Burden, 2000). The scale consists of twenty statements such as:

- "I know how to solve the problems that I meet";
- "When I'm given new work to do I usually feel confident I can do it"; and
- "Learning is difficult".

Respondents are required to indicate on a five point scale whether they definitely agree, agree somewhat, aren't quite sure, disagree somewhat or definitely disagree with each statement. A resultant overall score out of 100 can be compared with standardised norms to identify any individual's level of academic self concept. The scale can also be used to identify specific patterns of responses indicating perceived strengths and weaknesses. Ongoing research is beginning to reveal that many dyslexic people display a different pattern of responses to those with more general learning difficulties and that their overall scores are susceptible to change in both a negative and positive direction. This suggests that the MALS has value not only in the process of identification but also as a diagnostic indicator and a sensitive instrument to change.

Other scales are also available relating even more directly to the area of literacy. Amongst the most notable of these is the Chapman and Turner Reading Self Concept Scale. This scale, together with the MALS and several other self concept scales, are available in one package as part of the NFER-Nelson Self Concept Portfolio (Burden, 1998). Alternatively the MALS is available for independent purchase from NFER-Nelson.

Self Esteem

Self esteem differs from self concept in that it adds an evaluation dimension, i.e. it relates not only to how we make sense of ourselves and our situations but also to how we feel about it.

One way of considering self esteem is to see it as a measure of the difference between how we see ourselves and the kind of person we would like to be. The greater the distance between our actual self concept and our ideal self concept, the lower our feeling of self esteem.

Some researchers have focused explicitly on self esteem because they believe that how we feel about ourselves is the most important component of success in life. A notable contributor to this area is Denis Lawrence (1988) who has constructed several self esteem scales accompanied by suggestions for improving the self esteem of those who score poorly. Another contribution to this area is the Big Steem Scale of Maines and Robinson, published by Lucky Duck Corporation.

Psychological theories seeking to explain successful achievement have produced several constructs relating directly to self esteem. Amongst the most useful of these are the constructs of self efficacy, locus of control and learned helplessness. These are not easy constructs to measure but they are particularly important for teachers of dyslexic students. This is because it has been shown that underachievers are prone to feelings of learned helplessness which can lead to depression and that positive achievement is related of self efficacy (i.e. our confidence in achieving successful outcomes) and locus of control (whether we feel that what happens to us is in our own hands or in the control of powerful other people or forces). Recent research (Burden and Burdett, 2004) has shown that these constructs are particularly important contributors to the achievement of dyslexic people, that they are accessible to measurement and that they can be positively affected by the ethos of the school attended. It is anticipated that ways of assessing these aspects of self esteem will be made available in my book to be published by Whurr shortly.

References

Burden, R L (2000) "The Myself as a Learner Scale" (MALS). Windsor: NFER-Nelson.

Burden, R L (1998) "Self Concept Portfolio". Windsor: NFER-Nelson.

Burden, R L and Burdett, J W G (2004a). "Factors associated with successful learning in dyslexic students": *British Journal of Special Education* (in press).

Burns, R B (1982) "Self Concept Development and Education". London: Holt, Rinehart and Winston.

Bryne, B M (1996) "Measuring Self Concept across the Life Span". Washington: American Psychological Association.

Humphrey, N and Mullins, P M (2002) "Personal constructs and attributions for academic success and failure in dyslexia". *British Journal of Special Education*, 29(4), 196–203

Lawrence, D (1988) "Enhancing Self esteem in the Classroom". London: Paul Chapman.

Part 3

Managing Dyslexia in Adults

Dyslexia Support in Industry: Hairdressing

Teresa Mullin

The Dyslexic Person in Hairdressing

Career pathways that rely heavily on written communication methods can present barriers for dyslexic learners who may prefer using oral communication techniques. Vocations such as hairdressing (including barbering), that value oral communication skills, offer a dyslexic person a career route that recognises their preferred communication method. By choosing a career pathway which reduces the impact of a disability rather than highlight it, a dyslexic person with effective oral communication skills can attain personal excellence in their chosen career.

Industry Characteristics

The hairdressing and beauty therapy industry in the UK is estimated to employ over 200,000 people. It is an industry that continues to grow and attract recruits of all ages. In recent years it has been further popularised by the advent of celebrity hairdressers on television makeover programmes, dramas such as 'Cutting it' and the 'fly on the wall' documentary, 'The Salon'. Communicating with clients, colleagues and visitors to the salon form the foundation upon which this people-based, service industry is based. Of course, from a practical skills perspective, hairdressers must also acquire good organisational skills, creativity and dexterity and the ability to work well in a team. Where a dyslexic person has developed these personal attributes in addition to their practical hairdressing skills they can achieve their personal potential in a creative environment.

Expected Signs and Symptoms of a Hairdresser with Dyslexia

There are many signs and symptoms of developmental dyslexia which have been recognised as causing unusual difficulty. These include reading, spelling, writing, speech (occasionally), digits and numbers, sequencing, memory, orientation and specific tasks (e.g. tying shoelaces). All of these impact on the learner in employment. However, the ability of the dyslexic to be able to 'take control' of their environment is an important factor in reducing the stress of dyslexia and ultimately achieving employment success.

The following table illustrates some of the shared characteristics of my experience in training hairdressers who have had dyslexia.

Strengths	Weaknesses
Good verbal communication skills Good relationships with clients Creative, practical skills Often visual and kinaesthetic learners	Dexterity difficulties in developing skills Memory problems Remembering instructions Methods of work/ techniques Mixing instructions Slow to learn and understand Slow to achieve Low in confidence Easily stressed

The above strengths have also been recognised by Thomson (2002, p.2) who found that many people with dyslexia are better at 'gestalt' or three-dimensional and visualisation skills. Where a learner's natural talents can be incorporated into vocational work such as hairdressing the ability of the dyslexic to be able to 'take control' of their environment is further increased.

How to Become a Qualified Hairdresser or Barber

In order to qualify as a hairdresser a learner generally follows a National Vocational Qualification (NVQ) in Hairdressing course of study at a college of further education or a recognised learning provider. Where learners are based in a work-based learning environment (WBL) the NVQ often forms the basis of a Modern Apprenticeship (MA) programme.

An MA programme additionally requires the completion of Key Skills in Application of Number and Communication and more recently a Technical Certificate. Much of the coursework necessary to achieve an MA requires that the dyslexic must develop not only their practical skills, but also their 'key skills' to an industry-wide acceptable level of attainment.

It has been estimated that the proportion of young people with additional learning needs (ALN) recruited to hairdressing foundation MA courses is 9 per cent, almost double the rate across all vocational areas. Furthermore the level of dyslexic students who enter hairdressing is also higher than other vocations. Given the high reliance and value given to written forms of assessment and the high numbers of ALN learners in hairdressing, it is no surprise to learn that many apprentices do not achieve the key skills element of their apprenticeship framework.

Practical Ways to Provide Support

For learning providers and tutors there are various ways to support the dyslexic learner and enable them to achieve. Strategies can be as simple as making sure learners have access to a computer upon which to word process their written assignments. For others it may involve increased amounts of both vocational and specialist dyslexic support. Whatever strategy is chosen, it is essential that the initial identification of dyslexia triggers appropriate support measures being put in place. These are some suggestions:

- During initial assessment, identify the individual's learning needs and preferred learning style and discuss them with learner.
- Apply to the Learning and Skills Council (LSC) for funding to have an educational assessment completed for the learner.
- Apply for any available additional funding and, where possible, provide the learner with 1:1 specialised support.
- Work with the employer to identify situations or tasks that may cause stress to the learner and work on ways to increase the learner's strengths.
- Reduce alienation of peers by ensuring that all tutors are aware of the learner's preferred learning style, strengths and weaknesses so as not to cause embarrassment, for example by being asked to read aloud in a group.
- For assessment purposes allow the learner, where possible, the choice to complete assessments orally rather than in written form.
- Where possible allow the learner access to information technology for preparation of written material.
- Apply for 'extra time' or a 'reader' to the awarding body for written test assessment.

- Be available to the learner to talk over areas of difficulty.
- Work together with all stakeholder partners, particularly the employer, to support the learner.

The Disability Discrimination Act 1995 has recognised dyslexia as a disability. In work based learning, this means that funding can be accessed for an educational assessment and continued individual support for learners on LSC funded programmes. In this way dyslexic learners are encouraged to take control of their environment, their confidence increases, and their stress reduces. Support measures need to be continually evaluated throughout a course in terms of whether the additional support being provided continues to be appropriate for a learner and that progress is being made.

The Future for Dyslexics in Hairdressing

As the framework for achieving an MA expands, with higher levels of Key Skills requirements and the introduction of Technical Certificates, so too are the barriers which prevent the dyslexic hairdresser taking control of their environment. In an industry built on effective oral communication skills and practical creative ability, there is a concern that entry to the industry will become accessible only to learners who can achieve the written elements of funded programmes. As an industry, we must ask ourselves:

- Are we alienating a very important learner group by focusing on the mismatched set of values for our industry?
- In raising standards through emphasising the value of the written, standardised assessment route are we also raising 'barriers'?
- Are we creating an unequal opportunity?

In raising the profile of the hairdressing and industry, these are questions that must be considered by practitioners and the Consumer Services Industry Authority (CSIA) which represents the industry at national level.

References

Chief Inspectors report 2003 Hairdressing and beauty therapy – summary 'Context and trends'.

Kirk, J and Reid, G. (2003) Adult dyslexia checklist – criteria and considerations, *The Dyslexia Handbook*, 2003.

Thomson, M.(2001) *The Psychology of Dyslexia, A Handbook for Teachers*, Whurr Publishers, London.

Fitzgibbon, G. and O'Connor, B.(2002) *Adult Dyslexia, A Guide for the Workplace*, Wiley, Chichester, UK.

HABIA Research Statistics 1999

Partnership Work in Greenwich

Sue Sexton, Greenwich Action Team

The British Dyslexia Association (BDA), together with the North Kent Dyslexia Association (NKDA), has signed a service level agreement to work in partnership with the Greenwich Action Team (GAT). They are funded by JobCentre Plus as an outreach team.

The Greenwich Action Team supports unemployed clients living within the most disadvantaged wards in the Greenwich Borough. The Action Team Advisers work in some of the most deprived estates in South East London, working from premises within these estates, local partnership offices, a mobile unit which visits various sites in the Borough, and Belmarsh Prison.

The partnership between BDA, NKDA and GAT was formed in order to support the Dyslexia Friendly LEA Initiative. It aims to provide a unique one to one dyslexia friendly adviser service. This will adapt itself to the students' individual needs. The aim is for the partnerships to build up a rapport with the SENCo and students by talks or workshops for any students with literacy difficulties who wish to attend. They will also have the benefit of follow up visits by the same advisers, all of whom have a high level of personal commitment and knowledge of dyslexia. The students also have the consistency of being able to contact their advisers and gain knowledge of further education, university and job opportunities.

We all feel that this is a great opportunity to enable those students, who may not be reaching their full potential, to be aware of all their options and to have the opportunity to realise their true abilities.

The service will provide dyslexia aware advisers who also have extensive knowledge of the job market and other local support groups. The Partnership will also work with local employers to encourage them to take an active role in engaging school leavers, especially those who may have little or no paper qualifications but have obvious abilities to offer.

Again, this will be tailored to individual needs but will need the co-operation of companies who can offer modern apprenticeships and trainee positions with an emphasis on creative positions. When a student has a position to start within a company there will be further on-the-job support for the student and his or her employer.

The BDA can arrange training sessions for large employers and training packs for smaller companies. The NKDA and GAT can provide support on any on-the-job strategies that the trainee may need and weekly visits to ensure that employer and trainee are progressing together.

The partnership has already worked together to produce posters and a covering letter to go into the Dyslexia Friendly LEA packs addressed to the headteacher and SENCO in each secondary school. They have also produced "adviser friendly tips" in the style of bookmarkers, which can then be distributed to all south east London JobCentre Plus offices.

The partnership will be attending the local Chamber of Commerce meetings but would also welcome the opportunity to meet with any employers reading this article to discuss trainee positions and funding arrangements. Please call Sue Sexton on 07779 356 528 for further information.

ADSHE – Uniting Dyslexia Specialists in Higher Education

Ellen Morgan, Co-ordinator, Dyslexia Support Unit, City University

The last two years have seen the birth and launch of a valuable new resource for specialists involved with dyslexia in adults. The Association of Dyslexia Specialists in Higher Education (ADSHE) developed in response to a burgeoning number of dyslexic students entering HE, coupled with institutional response to the legal responsibilities set out in Part IV of the Disability Discrimination Act (DDA), also known as the Special Educational Needs Disability Act, 2001 (SENDA). Although many universities and other HE institutions had implemented some provision for dyslexic students during the 1990s, the DDA, Part IV, highlighted the urgency to institute appropriate provision to meet the varying needs of dyslexic students across the sector. Despite the existence of many concerned and active organisations, such as the BDA, the Dyslexia Institute, PATOSS and Skill, there was no organisation whose primary focus was to ensure that HE institutions offered their dyslexic students the assurance that reasonable adjustments would be made to allow them to reach their potential.

The Beginnings

In October 2001, in response to an email invitation, a group of Dyslexia Co-ordinators and specialist dyslexia tutors met at City University in London to share their concerns and experiences. They discussed common problems occurring in their respective institutions and identified the obstacles they encountered in response to their desires to meet student demands. Twenty five people attended the initial meeting and the enthusiasm expressed by many of those present impelled the group to call a second meeting. Initial meetings, which occurred roughly bi-monthly, attracted new and different representatives; indeed, as word spread, several people from further afield in England asked if they could attend meetings. The informality of these initial sessions gave way to the birth of ADSHE.

Objectives

Prior to the advent of the DDA, Part IV, prospective university students who knew they were dyslexic and had the benefit of diagnosis at school, had to research the provision available at different universities. This ranged from finding out whether they would be given examination accommodations, such as extra time, to discovering whether any individual tutorial support was available. It was a daunting task to sift through the widely varying provision, often resulting in choosing an institution based on the availability of support rather than selecting a university which offered the appropriate course. In some cases, students felt so despondent that they opted not to pursue their desire to obtain a higher qualification.

Those students who had not been identified in their school days often gained entry to HE through non traditional routes, such as Access courses, only to find that the problems which had interfered with their earlier academic success came back to haunt them. Many of these students, who may have been nurtured through the FE courses, confronted failure in HE as a result of the lack of appropriate support.

Clearly, legislation has had a major impact in terms of forcing institutions to examine their provision and to ensure that all students are given an equal opportunity to succeed. The general increased awareness of dyslexia and related Specific Learning Difficulties (SpLDs) has helped to overcome the lack of recognition many students experienced in the past and the sense of isolation felt by those who had been identified. The implementation of legislation has underpinned the determination of those, both staff and students, who have been committed to levelling the playing field between students with SpLDs and their colleagues.

In response to the changed climate, ADSHE's constitution set forward the following objectives:

1 To act as a forum for discussion of the professional interests of dyslexia specialists in Higher Education and to represent the professional and related interests of ADSHE members.

2 To share knowledge and disseminate good practice, including promoting and developing the understanding of all aspects of dyslexia.

3 To clarify and promote students' entitlement to dyslexia support within individual institutions and throughout the sector.

4 To promote understanding of disability legislation in relation to students with dyslexia.

5 To provide a professional viewpoint to relevant bodies such as the DfES and HEFCE on matters relating to HE students with dyslexia.

Early Days to the Present

ADSHE has made a swift progression from its first informal meeting in 2001. It has developed a website (www.adshe.org.uk) and first 'went public' at two dyslexia conferences in June 2003 at the Universities of Leicester and Hull. ADSHE had its official launch in March 2004 at the BDA International Conference at the University of Warwick. The launch generated extraordinary interest, with over 100 people in attendance, and a surge of membership in direct response, confirming the group's feeling that there is, indeed, a need for yet another association.

Membership is growing daily, and colleagues from abroad have expressed interest in joining; there are currently two 'associate member institutions' from overseas. Discussions on a large variety of topics are conducted through a closed JISC-mail discussion group, available only to members. Current membership is over 75 individuals, representing more than 50 institutions and including many freelance tutors who value the opportunity to 'meet' colleagues, either in person or through JISC-mail, thus overcoming the sense of isolation previously characteristic of support work in this field. The proliferation of members across Great Britain has resulted in the formation of several regional subgroups, making participation of ever increasing numbers possible.

The Future

ADSHE was conceived as an active organisation of concerned and committed professionals, all of whom share an interest specifically in the provision of support for dyslexic students in HE. It sees itself as a proactive association; that is, it does not simply want to meet to exchange ideas and to reinvent the wheel, it wants to harness the wide ranging experience and expertise of its diverse members to develop a national approach to meeting the needs of the students with whom we work. Although ADSHE is not a policy-making organisation, it hopes to be able to influence policy makers. After all, who better could contribute to policy decisions than those whose experiences and wisdom derive from working at the grass roots level? In recognition of its collective expertise, ADSHE has gained representation on a DfES committee, and has been consulted for advice and opinions, such as decisions being taken by external examining groups whose remit is outside the sphere of the universities, but lies within professional bodies.

ADSHE has opened a dialogue with the BDA and is working collaboratively with the Education Director.

One of the main hopes of ADSHE is to be able to harness the expertise of its many members to produce Guidelines for Good Practice. As these develop, they will be published on the website to be used as a reference by less experienced practitioners who want to ensure that their institutions are offering fair accommodations to their dyslexic students. By developing, agreeing and publicising good practice guidelines, ADSHE will make it possible for all institutions to achieve 'dyslexia friendly' environments and dyslexic students will be guaranteed a minimum level of support regardless of where they study.

Living with Dyslexia and Developing Coping Strategies

Barbara Riddick

One of the most fundamental things anyone with dyslexia has to do is to learn to live in a non dyslexic world. A world that expects certain standards of reading, spelling, co-ordination and remembering. Finding effective ways to cope is obviously a process of development which is influenced by a whole range of factors including, age, role, circumstances, personality, severity of dyslexia and so on. The coping strategies of a five year old struggling to learn to read will be different to those of an adult taking on a more managerial role at work that involves higher literacy demands.

Overcoming or Avoiding

Despite the seemingly very different requirements at various ages there are some basic aspects to coping strategies. Some are about finding a way round or avoiding a difficulty whereas others are about learning skills in order to overcome the difficulty. A common example with younger dyslexic children is the difficulty lots of them have in tying up shoe laces. Many parents solve this problem by buying shoes with Velcro fastenings, whereas some parents spend extra hands-on time teaching their child how to tie laces. The first is clearly a way round the problem whereas the second tackles the problem head on by teaching new skills. There are costs and benefits to both approaches. I now have a 20 year old dyslexic son who walks round with his shoe laces permanently undone because I chose the Velcro route. But in the primary school he was struggling with very severe dyslexia in a hostile school environment and all his energy was needed to cope with the day to day reading, writing and spelling demands of the classroom. The Velcro option was sensible at the time; learning to tie shoe laces was not a priority and it was one less skill that he had to learn. So at any age or stage there are decisions to be made about how much energy and resources should be put into coping with a range of different demands.

Manageable Coping Strategies

For day to day tasks, ideal ways of coping should take up as little time and attention as possible. In school, dyslexic children are often working against the clock because they need longer to do the same amount of reading and writing as other children. In secondary school my son was constantly told off by teachers for not having underlined his work, despite the fact that I often bought him rulers and put them in his bag. Even I thought he should be able to do this, so in exasperation I went out and bought 6 rulers, but still no underlining took place. But a heart to heart chat revealed the source of the problem. He was always under so much pressure to try and write sufficient down that stopping even for a precious minute or two to rummage round in his overflowing bag (often with no success) was more than he could cope with. A compromise was reached. A bag with an outside slot for his ruler was bought, and teachers only required him to underline the main title in class.

This example brings up an important issue. How far should a dyslexic person be expected to cope and how far should it be down to the rest of the world to adapt their demands or practices?

The Balance of Coping Strategies

Parents sometimes need to act as advocates for their children in negotiating a reasonable balance. It is important that children learn what should not be avoided, such as learning to read, and what may be optional, such as learning multiplication tables by heart. The balance of coping strategies will differ considerably depending on how many demands someone is trying to deal with and the relative importance of the different demands. Part of coping may be deciding which things to put on hold, and which things to work on at a given time.

At various points parents, children and adults with dyslexia have to make decisions about changing strategies, perhaps because something isn't working, the time or personal costs are too great, or other solutions have become available. By his early teens it became clear that, despite extra tuition and the delights of the school handwriting club, my son's illegible and painfully slow handwriting was not improving significantly for the amount of effort put in. Switching to largely word processing, with the blessing of the school, and taking an evening class in keyboard skills was a sensible change in coping strategy.

Developing Coping Strategies

Coping is an art which involves a blend of practicality, intuition, creativity, knowledgeability, determination and self-insight. Both children and adults with dyslexia unconsciously develop a variety of coping strategies many of which are positive but some of which can be negative. Parents and teachers play a vital role in helping children to develop a balanced range of strategies which are suited to their circumstances and individual personality. When I interviewed dyslexic children about their coping strategies in school, many said that they often avoided words they could not spell, whereas a few of the more confident

children said they always chose the word they wanted to use irrespective of whether they knew how to spell it or not (Riddick 1996). For some children this was the first time they had consciously discussed the various coping strategies they used. Others were aware of their strategies but were ashamed or frightened to reveal them. They needed the reassurance that it was OK to talk about what they did and that plenty of other dyslexic children did likewise.

Helping children with coping strategies can often go on in a practical understated way, but as children grow older it is sometimes useful to discuss and review them in a more open way. In school it may be possible to do this through a child's IEP (Individual Education Plan). One child who always avoided words she could not spell agreed to tell her teacher some of the more common ones. She then ranked which of these words she would most like to be able to use and had the top ranked word written on a card and stuck on her desk. She also agreed, in collaboration with her parents, to learn how to spell this word. Another child had an agreement with her teacher that the teacher would signal clearly whether she wanted her to be as accurate as possible or use as wide a range of words as possible. Helping children in this way gets over the message that solutions can be found to difficulties.

When coping is mentioned, practical support and strategies often spring to mind but social and emotional support should not be underestimated. Successful adults with dyslexia say that one of the most important factors in their success was that as children their parents believed in them (Scott, Scherman & Phillips 1992). If children have picked up negative messages from school or have made negative comparisons with other children it is often their parents who counter these. Probably the most important message for anyone with dyslexia is that they can cope and that solutions can be found to most problems.

References

Living with Dyslexia. Riddick, B. (1996) London, Routledge.

Helping individuals with dyslexia succeed in adulthood. Scott, M. E., Scherman A. & Phillips, H. (1992) *Journal of Instructional Psychology*. 19, 3

rockpoolreader

Jon Adams

I am the rock pool reader,
Sitting, heron style
        Hovering,
        Watching,
As the words move and shimmer,
        Back and forth
Floating in mid-water.
Each letter reaching its own perfect depth.

We reverse in the undertow,
        Side to side,
Gently swimming with the tidal flow.

Slowly but firmly spinning,
        Tightly gripped,
Held for ransom.
Never regaining a static position
But constantly positioned at random.

I am a rock pool reader,
Sitting, heron style.
        Hovering,
        Watching, as the
Concentric rings of light
Dance over banded limpet,
Weaving, entrancing the still Grey stone.
Forming an index with refractive alphabets.

Working with Dyslexia

Fiona Zinovieff

Throughout my extended college career (BA and PhD) I evolved my own ways of working. To some extent I even developed the confidence to defend these methods. However that was because I knew they worked in that environment. When I left academia for a post in a government organisation, it felt that yet again good spelling equates with ability and I felt stripped naked of my ruses and strategies.

People and Places

I have never been good at names, and here I was placed in a situation where I had to learn masses of people's names and also their job titles. There was no telephone sheet so I couldn't crib off that because everyone's contact details were all on the intranet – I couldn't access their details, as I didn't know their names to start with. For years I have carried a small hardbound notebook with me as a sort of external memory, so now I made a point of writing down people's names and job titles and notes about where they worked or what they might expect from me or to do for me. Initially I was doing this privately, but eventually I found that most people are quite flattered by the interest and so it never seemed to be taken as a weakness! I also added other details that would help me remember them, although these might not always have seemed so flattering! Many of my revision strategies came back into practice – so I learned that Julie had the 'jewely' picture frame on her desk and Mr. Hardy shared an unmistakable similarity with Oliver Hardy. I also drew a little chart of the immediate hierarchy in which I was working so that I knew who I should approach with problems or requests. I later found out that this is good management practice and is actually presented as an exercise in several courses!

I have learned to navigate myself around towns and even in the hills by relating places to landmarks. This does not work so well in large buildings – however, I do find that trying to keep my bearings with relation to the front of the building helps me set off in the right direction for the exit at home time! In the course of my work in different jobs I have had to visit many labyrinthine colleges and hospitals. If I have to meet someone I always ask for explicit directions and write them down and stick them into my diary. If I can, I ask at the reception and, if possible, get them to telephone to get someone to meet me. If I find that I have to spend some time working in a new place, I try setting myself a variety of small missions and wander around looking purposeful until I have mentally mapped the most important places. I find corridors confusing so I do try to notice some distinguishing feature, especially where they join.

When making train journeys I always print out the route details or get a copy at the ticket office. If I am driving somewhere unfamiliar I study the map first – and then I write out a list of the towns I am travelling through (and in brackets other towns on the same road). I try to guess what the road signs might say: for example, M5 south or the North West. Then I buckle my seatbelt and prepare to go round all the roundabouts three times reading the signs!

Time Management

In my first job I was given a diary which eventually became my greatest accomplice in the efficiency masquerade. It was one of those A5 diaries with a whole week across two pages. Through trial and error I learned to carry it with me at all times at work and to take it home with me in the evenings. In my work I often have to travel throughout the country meeting people, and so I learned to record not only the names and addresses of the people I was meeting but also their contact details for the day of the appointment. I also make a note of anything I should take with me – and if this is something I need to prepare I enter the task in my diary. For example if I was going to be away for a few days the entry for my last day in the office might say:

> "Print report for G.A., get tape-recorder and tapes – check batteries, book accommodation, print map."

I try to leave enough time between appointments for getting lost and for refreshing myself on the reasons for the meeting – actually writing the times down really helps me plan my time. At first I tended to leave my diary at work but I find it really useful for checking in the morning if I need to be smart, or to leave earlier than usual. Also I find it reassuring to know that if I am going to be delayed I can let the right people know. Even more reassuring is that everybody uses diaries!

When I first landed in the workplace I found the need to be accountable for my time very disconcerting! I have often found that apparently small tasks take an unexpectedly large amount of time – maybe this is because I tend to equate small with easy and so fail to notice how many steps they involve, or maybe it is because I tend to do them when I am at a low ebb and so performing at my worst. However, the old strategy of breaking tasks down into their component parts is wonderful especially if you then put these smaller tasks onto a sheet headed 'To do list'. I regularly use to-do lists to encourage me because I can see progress and other people can see what I am doing. I can plan my time better because I can see how many small steps there are to a given task. It also helps me manage my more dyslexic moments without sinking into a slough of despair about it. For example I can choose easier tasks such as making phone calls or photocopying when reading a large document might be too challenging.

Paperwork

On the spelling front, obviously first of all I got the spelling and grammar checker turned on – no spelling checker in the e-mail meant that I composed most of my e-mails in the word processor and then cut and pasted. I asked my boss if she would check any final documents for me. I think that asking in the right way is important as although she was aware of my problem she was not sure what she should do about it. It is important to be explicit about the kind of help and feedback you want and to be brave if there are more corrections than you initially anticipated. It often proves to be a useful way of working as two heads are usually better than one and quite often she had suggestions about the form or content as well as spelling mistakes.

Because I have had to learn to organise what I write, I use the outline view to build up a skeleton of the piece with various headings and sub-headings; this helps me stick to the point and present material in a more logical sequence. I have since found that this has an added advantage as it can be used as a discussion list when collaborating with other people. I also use it to make notes prior to meetings that can then be altered very easily to make a record of these meetings.

I have also learned when submitting expense forms that it is in my interests to take them in personally and have all those boxes checked – because otherwise it only comes back to me to fill in some omission or correction!

Finally

A new job or a new workplace presents new challenges for everyone and this is especially true for dyslexic people. It seems to me that the stresses in starting a new job make for greater feelings of vulnerability and these do not sit easily with the desire to give a good impression of competence for the role. I have made the decision to come clean about my dyslexia from the start. When I took up my most recent post I was put in touch with an organisation called Access to Work. Following an assessment they provided me with software, a recorder, a scanner and, best of all, a large monitor, so that I can enlarge all the electronic documents that I work with, which I found to be extremely helpful.

In my experience, although the problems of dyslexics are more severe and diverse than those of their non dyslexic colleagues, very few if any are entirely unique and 'owning up' to them often results in confessions of similar weaknesses in others. However, admitting to a problem is not a solution in itself – and many of us like to keep our darkest fears and secrets to ourselves – but identifying a specific problem is the first step to dealing with it.

Take Time
Movement exercises for parents, teachers and therapists of children with difficulties in speaking, reading, writing and spelling.
Mary Nash-Wortham
&
Jean Hunt
Dabbi

Sula Ellis
Tony Ellis
Jackie Davison
Mick Davison
Lifeboat
Book 1
Launch the Lifeboat to Read and Spell
Lifeboat Book 1
The Robinswood Press

SPOTLIGHT ON BLENDS
Gillian Aitken
Book One
Initial
Consonant Blends
The Robinswood Press

Sticks and Stones

Jonathan Adams BSc, Multimedia Artist and Poet

I went to school is less educationally enlightened times and wasn't called dyslexic. The primary school teachers had other words to describe me and the children had other words to give me. These words have stayed with me for 30 years, heavy words, cutting words, cruel words, such as "stupid" and "retarded".

> "Sticks and stones may break my bones but words will also get me"

Whatever you learn at school stays with you and the words that were thrown at me have interwoven into my personality. I've learnt a healthy respect and thirst for words, although I used to fear them; after all it was the words that used to get me into trouble. To me, words are physical, sharp, harmful and once seemed too dangerous to use.

> "Write me words
> that smell of blood between your lips,
> caught,
>   as you run your tongue
> along the imperfections of cracked glass
> feeling for indifference!"

From *Write Words*. Jonathan Adams, 2003
(See page 219 for full poem)

Now it seems ironic that I write, manipulating those very same hated objects, translating my experiences for others to understand and feel. If I can't find a suitable phrase I design one. Being able to move people through spoken and written words still seems very alien.

At school I did everything possible rather than speak out loud. I developed learned strategies, mostly negative, in case I was chosen to read. Sometimes these involved 10 different alternative scenarios, leaving me mentally exhausted, always expecting the worst. It was always the lack of strategy 11 that took me by surprise and really hurt.

From an early age I knew I was different, with a vivid imagination, continuously drawing and building model kits often without instructions. An average, normal, bright child enjoying the company of other children and adults. My last year at primary school did most damage and, by the age of 11, I was convinced I was worthless and stupid.

One particular teacher sat the girls in front and they would turn round laughing at those unfortunate enough to gain the teacher's attention. You learnt to sit still, not catch his glance otherwise he would pick on you, mercilessly exploiting any weakness you had. Mine was spelling and the humiliation would last well into the night, coming back as recurring nightmares. I would do my best to draw well as a cover for my stupidity but invariably this teacher would find a hole to exploit.

One time he deliberately spoilt an opportunity to have my work hung in the hall entrance by insisting I wrote my name and subject at the bottom. I spelt it wrong and my work was torn up, with satisfaction for a gladiatorial audience. He often started with soft words, full of implied sarcasm and then books would fly your way and the humiliation would physically sting. Each and every day I was ritually informed of my stupidity and worthless future. At first I hated him but eventually learned to internalise the anger; acceptance was better than fighting the pain.

"Sit still!
Don't catch his eye!
Stay invisible in the clear trout stream.
Even if you think he *will* see you.
Stare intently,
reading the patterns on the dull wooden desk,
as the lines flow and form,
constantly morphing.
        Absorbing?
Taking all your concentration
away from the departing words,
that run, scared all over your pages
of hand drawn neutral camouflage.
Wear your bullet proof jacket
with the heart shaped hole!
        Snared?
Cornered scapegoat!
Released into your desert playground
with each child's burdens on your back."

From *Betrayal fish*. Jonathan Adams, 2001

I sat at my desk, daydreaming, creating landscapes populated by sharks, dinosaurs, anything to escape the embarrassment. For the rest of my life the best strategy was to hide. People hurt you, underlining the deficiencies you had in front of the many.

After stumbling through university and gaining a degree, mainly by visualisation memory techniques, I turned to what I knew best: drawing. Unable to face working with others in case my "stupidity" showed I became self employed. It took a while to break into the publishing market as I was disabled by my lack of self-esteem and confidence; you can't tell someone you're great at drawing if you don't believe it yourself. I became obsessive about checking, as there could be no margin for error. I still retained hang ups about handing in work so avoided contact by letter and opted for face-to-face briefings with editors or designers. Soon I became successful at drawing for children's books, particularly 3D cutaway illustrations, and developed a good personal relationship with the editor and designers for the *See Through History* series of books. The pictures were seen by tens of thousands of children worldwide. At last I was in demand, accepted. Privately I couldn't feel I was achieving anything, that I had just fooled them into thinking I wasn't stupid and eventually I would slip up and be uncovered.

In late 1998 life unravelled. The book work ended, the editors and designers all left for other companies and I wasn't required any more. My self-esteem was rock-bottom from wrestling with my private life. Consequently I couldn't face writing to publishers, nor could I complete DSS forms to sign on, being terrified of getting into trouble.

Meanwhile my son had been confirmed dyslexic and a chance comment – a few words – turned everything on its head. I mentioned that "everything read as if it was underwater!" My son said the same. Was I dyslexic? What was dyslexia? Would it confirm that I was stupid? The next week I spoke with a dyslexic photographer at an exhibition and was advised to speak to the jobcentre Disability Employment Adviser. As my PACT assessment results were explained to me as "profoundly dyslexic – very spatially gifted", I wanted to cry. Here I was, at the age of 38, feeling 11 again. I had frozen, been trapped at that age for so long. Perversely I am glad I wasn't diagnosed at school as, in those days, there was precious little help available. I think it would have given me an excuse not to try. Endless lines writing "I can't because I'm dyslexic".

It was hard to come to terms with the realisation that I was abused at school. I couldn't draw as my hands, my life, were painful but felt compelled to express my feelings, work them through. I started to write, to transcribe feelings from pictures in my imagination into words. One of the first was *rockpoolreader* and, although I started to receive critical acclaim for this new work, life was still too furious for feelings. I made contact with the BDA through winning the "As I See It" competition two years running and was given the details of the Arts Dyslexia Trust who supported and encouraged me throughout this time. In early 2003 I felt my head break the surface, swimming, not struggling. I had been frightened of seeming stupid but certainly wasn't scared of being dyslexic.

I am the rock pool reader,
Sitting, heron style
    Hovering,
    Watching.
As the words move and shimmer,
    Back and forth.
Floating in mid-water,
Each letter reaching its own perfect depth.

From *rockpoolreader*. Jonathan Adams, 2000
(See page 206 for full poem)

The last taboo was broken when I was asked to recite for the Arts & Visual Thinking Conference, after the main meal, in Falmouth, 2003. I had to read aloud. I couldn't remember my own or any poetry rote fashion. However, by employing visualisation and marking the poems with symbols I was able to read word perfect. From the emotional comments and letters I received afterwards I knew this was something I would have to do again. I had moved people with words far more empathically than through drawing. My personal expression of working through the consequences of the abuse could touch others; it all had purpose. If it meant one person changed their opinion or felt they didn't have to hide I would stand and read in front of thousands. So, with help from Access to Work and Enham Ability I found myself self employed again as a multimedia artist and dyslexic poet.

I still have weaknesses; a few mis-chosen words can trigger a flashback. I'm there again, 11 years old, sitting at my desk, face down, waiting for the humiliation to start. Sometimes it's so real I can feel it, taste it, which is why I write based on tactile visual imagery. I do regret the abuse but I wouldn't exchange being a positive dyslexic or my "specific learning difference". Without it there would be no "words" for me to share.

Jon is currently illustrating several children's books, editing a book of poetry for the Arts Dyslexia Trust and working on a project combining words-music-video entitled "7 short films about dyslexia". He can be contacted at:

62 Old Road
Gosport
Hampshire
PO12 1RE
Tel: 023 9279 2021
www.rockpoolreader.co.uk

Write words

Jon Adams

Write me words
that smell of blood between your lips,
caught,
as you run your tongue
along the imperfections of cracked glass
feeling for indifference!

Write me words
that feel the weight of winter!
frozen as my fingers and tongue,
numb pronouncements,
spoiling for release in shallow ponds
dormant till spring.

Write me words
that I can never see!
blinded by frightened fissile flies
that fill my optic nerves,
manufactured from twisted uranium wires
and filled with humiliation.

Write me words
that taste of burning flesh!
drawn and calcined fingers
compelled to hold coals,
conducting degrees of embarrassment
designed to kill at 30 yards.

Specific learning difficulty

Jon Adams

Specific learning difficulty
copy these words off the board
just repeat after me
specific learning difficulty
separate me from this learnt incompetence

specific learning difficulty
no! don't do it like that its your stupidity
that same word again wrong deliberately
specific learning difficulty
isolate me from all teacher indifference

specific learning difficulty
no your getting it wrong this is really insane
just write it again and again and again
specific learning difficulty
withdraw me from your rote religiousness

specific learning difficulty
your just wrong again cant you see what I'm saying
why do you sit there like that in your permanent daydream
specific learning difficulty

please celebrate my creative ability
as I see more than you will ever know
feeling times smooth surface arc and flow
touching with hands of remembered imagination
walking neural paths with memory visualisation
my specific learning difference

Part 4

Policy

Dyslexia Friendly LEAs and Schools: The BDA Quality Mark Initiative

Susan Tresman, BDA Chief Executive and Education Director

This is a collaborative project which culminated in September 2004 with the launch of the pilot phase of the BDA Dyslexia Friendly LEA Quality Mark Initiative. It involves:

- BDA;
- LEAs;
- local dyslexia associations (LDAs);
- parents;
- learners; and
- schools.

This initiative builds on examples of good practice in schools and LEAs. Many have been working towards dyslexia friendly status and this project aims to forge a new strategic alliance with LEAs under the leadership of the BDA. A long period of consultation resulted in a framework for the BDA Quality Mark and this is now being rolled out in LEAs throughout England and Wales.

The Quality Mark Procedure

The vision is that the BDA, LDAs and LEAs can form a unique partnership. This will help address the challenges posed by the new SEN strategy document from the Government's *Removing Barriers to Achievement*. A series of elements of best practice for dyslexia friendly LEAs have been developed under four standards:

1 Leadership and Management.

2 Teaching and Learning.

3 Classroom Environment.

4 Partnership and Liaison with Parents, Carers, Governors and Learners.

LEAs are provided with guidance and documentation from the BDA that shows them how to undertake a self audit of their practice against those standards. Progress against the standards is self evaluated and then declared according to a continuum. LEAs will declare themselves as:

- focusing on an area;
- developing their practice;
- having established practice; or
- sharing enhanced practice, worthy of sharing beyond the LEA.

In all cases they will declare what evidence they have to verify their audit and where this is located.

LEAs can join the scheme and spend a maximum of two years working towards gaining the BDA Quality Mark. If they are not yet ready to apply, they are allocated a "buddy" LEA that already holds the Quality Mark to encourage them on their journey.

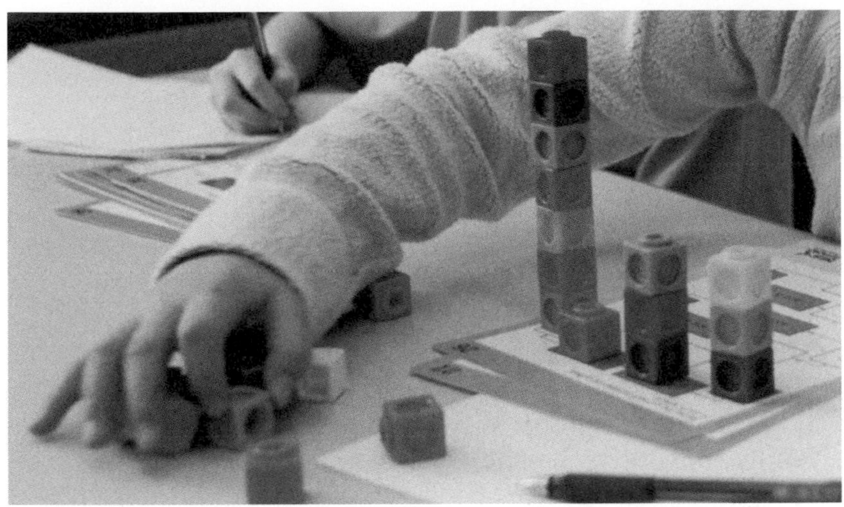

LEAs must submit the documentation and guidance to the BDA. A verification visit is then made by a Quality Marked LEA, during which any aspect of evidence listed by the LEA in the audit may be called for analysis. If all is in order the Quality Mark can be awarded.

Candidates for the Quality Mark will be expected to show a continuum of development and effectiveness against the standards in respect of the impact and quality of their provision for inclusive education. Particular reference should be made to dyslexia and identifying areas requiring improvement.

Award of the BDA Quality Mark

Overall, for the Quality Mark to be awarded, LEAs need to meet a number standards outlined in the BDA Dyslexia Friendly Standards documentation. They should not exceed the number of standards required in either the Focusing or Developing categories as follows:

- Focusing: No more than 6 standards
- Developing: No more than 9 standards
- Established: 12–15 standards
- Enhanced: 0–3 standards

In respect of the promotion and establishment of dyslexia friendly schools within and under the auspices of each LEA, a similar progression in the number of Quality Marked schools or those schools working towards attaining dyslexia friendly status is to be shown over time:

Schools within an LEA

For the initial Quality Mark to be awarded to an LEA:	20%
On re-recognition after the first three years:	35%
Second re-recognition (six years):	50%
Third re-recognition and beyond:	75–100%

BDA Quality Marks are valid for three years. After that time a re-recognition visit is undertaken using a system of peer mentors drawn from regional LEA groupings. Between recognition visits, LEAs will be expected to demonstrate progress in two areas: that is to say statements of practice in the Focusing category have moved to Developing. Those in Developing have moved to Established and so on. Therefore, by the third recognition visit in nine years time, 24 Standards in the Established category need to be met and 3 in the Enhanced category. Dyslexia friendly status must have been achieved by more than 75% of schools within the LEA.

Dyslexia Friendly Schools

As previously mentioned LEAs have a responsibility to challenge and develop dyslexia friendly status in their schools. To help them the BDA Quality Mark Initiative has been developed under the auspices of the same consultation group and the Exemplar School Standards, under the same four categories:

- Leadership and Management in Schools
- Teaching and Learning in Schools
- Classroom Environment
- Partnership and Liaison with Parents, Carers, Governors and Learners.

How to Join

LEAs join the Quality Mark Initiative by applying to the BDA Education Office for membership and paying an annual fee. They are then provided with the full Quality Mark service. This fee entitles members to a range of benefits, including:

- Administration of the Quality Mark.
- A buddy LEA to support their progress (if appropriate).
- Administration of the Re-recognition process.
- Peer mentoring verification visits.
- Conferencing opportunities at reduced rates.
- Occasional services of the BDA Education Director as speaker or to attend LEA events.
- Helpdesk facility within the Education Office at susant@bda-dyslexia.demon.co.uk.
- Networking opportunities.
- A free copy of the new edition of the Dyslexia Friendly Schools Information Pack, funded by the DfES.

We have invited approximately 25 LEAs to join the pilot. This group will include 10–12 LEAs who have make sterling contributions during the consultation period.

It is gratifying to see the enthusiasm and commitment that colleagues in the LEAs, local dyslexia associations and schools are directing towards this new project. The BDA are poised to come together to exert what we hope will be a significant impact on the inclusiveness of our LEAs, schools and classrooms for dyslexic students, for those with other specific learning differences and indeed for all learners.

Please come back in 2006 to read about what happened next in the next edition of the BDA Handbook!

Inclusive Education: Dyslexia Friendly LEAs and Schools

The following is the presentation to a lecture I gave at the 2004 Spring Council outlining our plans for the Quality Mark Initiative.

Further information about the Initiative can be found on the website at www.bda-dyslexia.org.uk.

If you would like an electronic copy of this article, please contact Kate Vose on katev@bda-dyslexia.demon.co.uk or telephone 0118 966 2677.

Susan Tresman
Chief Executive and Education Director
British Dyslexia Association

Inclusive Education:
Dyslexia Friendly LEAs and Schools

British Dyslexia Association
Registered Charity No: 289243

Inclusion: Core values

- New SEN strategy – sets out a wide range of proposals to assist schools on meeting this challenge
- Revised OFSTED Framework for Inspection of Schools – more emphasis on inclusion
- In order to be effective schools must be inclusive
- OFSTED inspection teams are required to make a judgement of this

British Dyslexia Association
Registered Charity No: 289243

Role of LEAs in supporting inclusion:

- Have duties to support school improvement to ensure needs of pupils are met
- Statutory duties in relation to identifying, assessing providing for children with SEN
- To publish information on SEN policies and plans for support of schools and pupils
- Under the School Standards and Framework Act 1998 to promote high standards for all including additional and special needs and those whose needs are provided for in mainstream classes by wave interventions

British Dyslexia Association
Registered Charity No: 289243

Audit Commission 2001

Barely half of LEAs systematically monitoring work of schools with regard to SEN and inclusion

British Dyslexia Association
Registered Charity No: 289243

What can the BDA and LEAs do in partnership to address the challenge?

British Dyslexia Association
Registered Charity No: 289243

- Many of the needs catered for in mainstream relate to literacy and numeracy difficulties
- Dyslexia – high incidence and the reason for many of these needs

British Dyslexia Association
Registered Charity No: 289243

Dyslexia – a definition:

- Dyslexia is a specific Learning Difference which is constitutional in origin (in the make up of the person) independent of socio-economic or language background, and can occur at any level of intellectual ability.
- It can cause unexpected and persistent difficulties in acquiring certain skills in one or more of the following areas:

  Reading, writing, spelling and sometimes numeracy and spoken language.
- There may be accompanying weaknesses in:

  speed of processing, short term memory, sequencing, motor skills audit or visual perception

British Dyslexia Association
Registered Charity No: 289243

In an inclusive world can we still talk specifically about dyslexia?

- Widely acknowledged that interventions that are good for dyslexic learners benefit all learners
- Input to inclusive agenda – from a range of specialised expertise and experience inform the bigger picture and identify valid generic approaches
- Voluntary sector in collaboration with Educational practitioners and government

British Dyslexia Association
Registered Charity No: 289243

THE VISION

☞ A BDA Quality Mark for LEAs

☞ LEAs Quality mark their own schools

British Dyslexia Association
Registered Charity No: 289243

A collaboration to realise the vision

- BDA
- Local Dyslexia Associations
- LEA Colleagues
- Schools
- Parents and Governors
- Advisory Group

British Dyslexia Association
Registered Charity No: 289243

- A strategic development group
- Concept defined by standards
- Working groups informing the strands
- Strands informing the Standards
- Monitoring standards – regional peer groups

British Dyslexia Association
Registered Charity No: 289243

What are areas in which the standards are being developed?

Four frameworks for action are planned

1. Leadership and Management
2. Teaching and Learning
3. Class Environment
4. Partnership and Liaison

British Dyslexia Association
Registered Charity No: 289243

1. LEADERSHIP and MANAGEMENT

- Planning
- Policy
- Targeting resources
- Supporting Professional development into practice

British Dyslexia Association
Registered Charity No: 289243

2. TEACHING and LEARNING

- Assessing impact of schools on SEN
- Measurable outcomes – advice to schools
- Provision of data to schools
- Supporting school improvement – a continuum of development

British Dyslexia Association
Registered Charity No: 289243

3. CLASSROOM ENVIRONMENT

- Supporting self-evaluation and review of practice

British Dyslexia Association
Registered Charity No: 289243

4. PARTNERSHIP and LIAISON

- Listening to and responding to views of children, parents
- Governors, Employers
- Partnerships in Excellence for Inclusivity

British Dyslexia Association
Registered Charity No: 289243

Set of standards for schools – guidance from BDA

Under same four frameworks for action:

1. Leadership and Management
2. Teaching and learning in School
3. Classroom environment
4. Partnership and Liaison

Around these parameters: Standards Negotiated Locally between LEA and School

British Dyslexia Association
Registered Charity No: 289243

4 stages envisaged in the progression to meeting the standards:

1. Focusing
2. Developing
3. Establishing
4. Enhancing

How are the standards monitored?

- At LEA level – peer review
- Regional consortia
- At School level
- By the LEA

British Dyslexia Association
Registered Charity No: 289243

The road map:

- Standards developed
- Participants in pilot sought
- Fees paid for year 1
- Documentation and resources to pilot LEAs
- LEAs Self audit against standards
- Quality marks awarded
- Begin process of Quality Marking schools
- Free resources from BDA to schools (support of DfES)

British Dyslexia Association
Registered Charity No: 289243

Benefits

1. Provision of standards framework document and documentation to facilitate self review and audit against the standards.
2. Provision of guidance on the system for obtaining the BDA Quality Mark and having it reviewed periodically.
3. Awarding the Quality Mark.
4. Provision of Free DfES sponsored resource pack.
5. Provision of communication and networking opportunities, seminars and conferences at reduced cost, email help desk from the BDA Education Office.
6. Opportunity to join a panel of peer-reviewers and engage in peer reviews of other Quality Marked LEAs on three year cycle.

British Dyslexia Association
Registered Charity No: 289243

Contact Details

Kate Vose
Education Manager
British Dyslexia Association
katev@bda-dyslexia.demon.co.uk
0118 929 6946 (office)

98 London Road
Reading
RG1 5AU
www.bda-dyslexia.org.uk

British Dyslexia Association
Registered Charity No: 289243

The Journey towards Dyslexia Friendly Schools in Cheshire

Anne McLoughlin, Dyslexia Friendly Schools Working Group, Cheshire LEA

In September 2004 all schools in Cheshire were invited to apply for the Dyslexia Friendly Schools Quality Mark. At the same time Cheshire submitted an application to the BDA to become Quality Marked.

The Beginning

There was a need in the county to review the policy on specific learning difficulties, drawn up in 1994, because it used an outdated model to identify dyslexia. It did not fit well with an equal opportunities approach to supporting children with literacy difficulties. A proposed new policy was drafted and presented to a Learning Support Service Meeting of the Senior Management Team in December 2000.

Around the same time the ideas around dyslexia friendly schools were emerging in other LEAs and the BDA provided a resource pack to help schools to become dyslexia friendly. In April 2001 a Dyslexia Friendly Schools Group was set up in Cheshire consisting of representatives from parents, parent partnership, school SENCOs, Educational Psychologists, Specialist Support Teachers, Statutory Assessment managers and the local dyslexia association. Cliff Warwick (SEN Adviser in Swansea at that time) spoke to the group about the Swansea Story. It became clear that dyslexia friendly schools were the way forward to include pupils with dyslexia in mainstream schools.

Next Steps

A small dyslexia friendly schools working group was set up consisting of teachers, educational psychologists, a Statutory Assessment Manager and representatives of the Cheshire Dyslexia Association, This group presented a paper to the Learning Support Service Senior Management Team in November 2001. It was discussed with the whole Learning Support Service in December 2001, and the Cheshire advisory service in February 2002. A consultation pack was sent out to all schools in September 2002 which included the Dyslexia Friendly Schools Paper. A display was presented to schools governors and parent partnership in October 2002. Members of the working group also held several meetings with SENCo network groups to inform them of the proposals and to receive feedback

Further Developments

- In December 2002 a small group was set up to develop the Dyslexia Friendly Schools Quality Mark.
- The training of teachers became an important component in the dyslexia friendly schools initiative. Cheshire has been training teachers for ten years through their Foundation Course (credited through Manchester Metropolitan University). Work was going on to provide a course with a higher qualification which would give teachers AMBDA Status. This course began in January 2004. In September 2004 a new course to train teaching assistants was introduced.

By Andrew Dodd
Wilmslow High School

- In parallel to the dyslexia friendly schools initiative, the new policy on individual literacy difficulties was finalised.
- The Dyslexia Friendly Schools Initiative was launched by the director of education and county inclusion manager to representatives from the local dyslexia association, head teachers, school SENCos, advisers, consultants, specialist support staff, and elected county councillors in January 2004.
- A pilot of the Quality Mark was completed in the summer term 2004.

- At every stage of this process professionals were consulted, the only group who had not yet been consulted were children. Therefore, all children in schools were invited to enter a competition to design a picture for the Dyslexia Friendly Schools Quality Mark application form. There was a good response and the children produced some very interesting ideas on what dyslexia means to them and what a dyslexia friendly school is. Many of the children's pictures will be included in the quality mark application form and the guidance book, and some are reproduced here.
- The chair of the dyslexia friendly schools group is also a member of the British Dyslexia Association Strategic Development Group which has introduced the BDA Quality Mark for LEAs.

- In July 2004 the criteria and evidence for the Dyslexia Friendly Schools Quality Mark in Cheshire were finalised and schools began to apply for dyslexia friendly schools status in September 2004

In Conclusion

The success of this initiative has been the result of collaborative working and consultation at every stage. Sharing of information with the BDA and other authorities has been invaluable. In Cheshire we recognise that the journey will be on ongoing for some time.

"I'm Glad that I Don't Take No for an Answer"

Parent-Professional Relationships and Dyslexia Friendly Schools

Carol Griffiths, Brahm Norwich and Bob Burden,
University of Exeter
Introduction by Carol Youngs

Introduction

This report arises from an action research project funded jointly by the British Dyslexia Association (BDA) and the Frank Buttle Trust. It started in late autumn of the year 2000 and ran for two years in five LEAs in the south-west region. Its focus was on action based approaches to address the problems facing parents when trying to establish and meet the needs of dyslexic children in school.

The BDA funded a development officer to advise and support parents who were experiencing difficulty in obtaining appropriate provision for their child whilst also promoting the idea of dyslexia friendly schools (DFS).

The Frank Buttle Trust funded a research fellow who was based at the School for Education and Life Long Learning at Exeter University who would carry out in depth case analyses of children as seen mainly through the eyes of their mothers, over a two year period.

In parallel with this, a second strand of research set out to monitor the demands made upon the time and expertise of the independent development officer appointed by the BDA.

Further details of both this summary and the full report are available on the BDA website at www.bda-dyslexia.org.uk/main/research

Background

The purpose of this research was:

- "to establish routes to develop best practice models of communicating with and advocating for parents"; and
- "to be of key importance in promoting effective partnership with parents and quality inclusive education for dyslexic children".

(Summary of Original Proposal, Buttle Trust and British Dyslexia Association, 2000).

In particular, we were anxious to find examples of good or even excellent practice whilst reflecting the perspectives of the central participants in this enterprise: the children, their parents, their teachers and Local Education Authority policy makers. A specific region of England was selected which included five neighbouring LEAs and information was sought on the policies of these with regard to identification of and provision for children with special educational needs in general and dyslexia in particular.

It was decided not to attempt a large scale survey of a representative sample of dyslexic children and their families, but carry out in-depth case analyses of children, as seen mainly through the eyes of their mothers, over a two year period. We considered that such an approach would be more likely to provide rich data about the interactions between families and schools, set within the wider contexts of LEA and government policies. In parallel with this, a second strand of the research set out to monitor demands made upon the time and expertise of an independent development officer appointed on a temporary part time contract by the British Dyslexia Association. In this way it became possible to gather data on the experiences of a further seven families with whom the development officer had worked over the two year time period.

A project research officer was appointed with considerable background experience in social research. She was given the responsibility of interviewing the following:

- Key policymakers within the five LEAs.
- A small sample of Special Educational Needs Co-ordinators (SENCOs) in schools demonstrating good practice
- The fourteen identified families

She also monitored the work of the development officer.

The results of these overlapping sets of investigations are highly complex, as is revealed in the main body of this research report. We assume that the process of education takes place within nested and overlapping contexts of families, schools, LEAs and wider government policies. We see the role of the research presented here as illustrating how each of these contexts affects the other and thereby providing pointers as to how children with dyslexia or any other form of special need can best be helped to achieve their full potential. The findings demonstrate that dyslexia is not a simple issue that can be overcome by the implementation of structured literacy programmes or even by impressive policy initiatives alone. Nor does it make sense to consider the needs of dyslexic children separately from those of other children with SEN or of children and families in general. Where examples of poor practice have been identified, it is clear that the issues raised are for the

most part not necessarily specific to dyslexic children alone but often reflect weaknesses in home-school relationships. In the last analysis, it is at the level of individual interactions between teachers and parents that a great deal of work still needs to be done.

Chapter Summaries

Chapter one begins with a consideration of the notion of partnership between schools and parents and dyslexia friendly schools. It reveals their complexity and a considerable amount of dissatisfaction across the country as a whole with regard to partnership in practice. It also reveals the paucity of research into home-school relationships with regard to dyslexic children.

Chapter two describes the methodology used in the research. This consisted of:

- four interviews carried out between Autumn 2001 and Spring 2003 with each of seven families of dyslexic children;
- an in-depth examination of the case histories of seven families who sought help from the development officer, all of whom were interviewed once in the Spring of 2002;
- interviews with officers from each LEA responsible for special needs policy;
- visits to two schools identified by LEA officers as representing examples of good practice;
- an examination of Ofsted reports on each of the schools and LEAs;
- visits to mainstream schools and an independent specialist school for dyslexic pupils;
- interviews with representatives of four local voluntary associations for the families of dyslexic children;
- interviews with the development officer and a BDA representative about their aims for the development aspect of the project;
- an analysis of the weekly logs of the development officer regarding her activities, together with a weekly telephone conversation to elaborate on or clarify the information given; and
- a final self-evaluation by the project research officer of her work.

Chapter three provides detailed information about the SEN policies implemented by each of the five LEAs with specific reference to provision for meeting the needs of dyslexic pupils. It brings together information from interview data, LEA documentation, national statistics about statements issued, special school placements and SEN tribunal appeals with aspects from the latest LEA Ofsted reports.

It is not the intention of this research to attempt to interpret this information as indicative of more or less supportive policies with regard to meeting the needs of dyslexic children and their families. What is abundantly clear, however, is the considerable variation that exists with regard to such policies and provision between LEAs within a relatively compact geographical area. The distance of just a few miles could mean the difference of being educated within an area with a long-standing, high level policy of support for children with special educational needs or one with no ostensible policy at all. It could be argued therefore, that one highly significant factor in receiving satisfactory support for their dyslexic child is likely to be a family's area of residence.

In **Chapter four** we provide an analysis of the main themes arising from the interviews with seven families who had established and maintained contact with the project development officer over the two year period. What emerges immediately from these interviews is the appreciation of the families concerned that a person had been found to exist in this or a similar role, independently from schools or the LEA, with whom they could share their concerns and from whom they could seek advice as to the best way forward. The importance of the independence of such a person from any vested interest other than to provide a listening ear and objective, knowledgeable guidance cannot be overestimated.

The specific themes arising from these interviews can be summarised briefly here as demonstrating a recurring pattern of:

- initial concern by parents, often single mothers, about their children's difficulties in coping with learning early in their school careers;

- a lack of or inadequate response from the children's schools;
- an escalation of the problem into the behavioural area often affecting siblings and other family members;
- perceived misjudgements of the children by their teachers; and
- growing confusion, frustration and anger in the parents coupled with a lack of knowledge about who to turn to for help or advice beyond the school gates.

It is here that broader LEA policies with regard to SEN support came sharply into focus and where knowledge provides power. Even where open referral systems exist to psychological services or other LEA officers, access to such information is by no means always readily accessible. It is here also that the application of a diagnostic label such as 'dyslexia' is often found by parents to help them make sense of their children's difficulties.

The role of the development officer here was not to make such a diagnosis but to help the parents establish contact with someone with the expertise to make this possible where appropriate. What became clear, moreover, is that this in itself is sometimes not enough. A diagnosis of dyslexia by an LEA or independent expert does not necessarily mean that appropriate action will be taken by the child's current or future school. Inadequate or missing IEPs or Statements of Special Needs can themselves lead to further frustration and disillusionment on the part of individual children and their families, again providing the necessity for ongoing support to parents who see themselves as in a constant battle with the education system which is not of their own making.

The analysis of the seven case histories of families is presented in **Chapter five**. It can be seen here that the problems faced by these families were similar in many respects to those described in Chapter four. The main difference here is that as these parents have not had access to what they would view as any form of adequate support, they have had to develop their own strategies for dealing with what they often saw as an escalating set of problems. In this chapter we have attempted to summarise the nature of such strategies and the way in which they begin to shape the parents' sense of identity as a 'dyslexic parent'.

Here again we see how early parental concerns, usually expressed by mothers, are often interpreted by teachers, as an overreaction. Where little or no progress is shown, the parents begin to lose faith in the school and look elsewhere for information about possible explanations and/or more effective teaching materials or process. If the school appears to be unwilling to communicate at this level, this can lead to a search for an alternative LEA school in the first instance. If this option is not viable, and access is denied to LEA, psychological or support services, an independent assessment may well be sought. This can of course be costly, which in itself provides a degree of legitimisation of any diagnosis or label which may arise. At this point a conflict of opinion may well begin to escalate into a power struggle between the parents and the LEA as to how the perceived needs of the child can best be met. Private tuition may be sought for the child or he/she may be withdrawn from the LEA school system and taught by the parents at home for a brief or longer period, often with the help of independent organisations such as the Dyslexia Institute. It is here that voluntary organisations such as the British Dyslexia Association and its local parent groups often have a significant part to play. A place at an independent school specialising in the education of dyslexic children may well now be sought with an appeal for LEA funding. The denial of such funding may well lead to an application for an appeal to the SEN tribunal and eventually to longer term opting out of the LEA system.

One of the major findings of this research is that such negative escalation of action by parents of dyslexic children is not necessary and may be prevented in the majority of cases by the application of respect, effective communication and appropriate action by teachers and LEA representatives.

That movement towards more effective LEA-School-Parent partnership can be aided by someone acting in the role of a development officer, as established within this project, is revealed in **Chapter six** of the report. It summarises the main reasons why parents of dyslexic children across the five LEAs felt it necessary to seek external advice and support from the development officer. Here it can be seen that perceived lack of information, inadequate or negative communication and lack of appropriate assessment and intervention top the list.

By far the most frequent form of intervention by the development officer took the form of providing information to parents about dyslexia, the SEN Code of Practice and the role of LEA officers such as educational psychologists. Often this could be dealt with within a single telephone conversation. Another frequent but fairly straightforward form of action was to put parents in contact with local support networks.

A more complex set of issues requiring sensitivity, tact and skills related to parents' need for advice on how to approach professionals at every level and for action as a 'critical friend' in mediating between teachers and LEA representatives even to the extent of accompanying the parents to formal meetings and/or even speaking and working on their behalf. Whilst there is strong anecdotal evidence that parental appreciation for the work of the development officer in this project was considerable, it is clear that taking on such a role is akin to being placed in the middle of a minefield.

It was not the remit of our research to investigate the nature of the power relationships existing between parents, schools and individual teachers, and LEA policy officers. However, it seems clear that the emergence of very highly vocal parent organisations, such as local BDA branches, has been as a result of feelings of disempowerment felt by the parents of children manifesting specific difficulties such as dyslexia. At the same time it seems highly unlikely that any LEA or very few schools will ever be able to reach a position where conflicts of aims, perceptions and priorities never arise. In such circumstances the existence of an objective outsider playing the part of an informed 'critical friend' can be invaluable, as we have seen here. The really difficult issue then becomes one of how such a person should be funded, trained and accepted within education system without being seen as a representative of one or other form of vested interest. All we can reliably say as a result of this project is that there is a perceived need amongst parents for someone to take on such a role, that there is more than enough work for someone undertaking such a role on a regional basis, and that it is possible for the right person to navigate the minefield to the general satisfaction of most parties involved, given respect on all sides.

In **Chapter seven** we summarise examples of good practice that were encountered by the development officer and the project research officer in the duration of the project. Taking into account the difficulties of identifying exactly what might constitute 'good' practice, we were able to identify a number of examples of interesting and promising LEA policies, positive organisational aspects of schools and interpersonal highs and lows. Our main finding here, which is hardly novel, is that good practice cannot and should not exist in isolation, but in the last analysis will stand or fall at the level of personal interactions. By this we mean that it is obviously vitally important for LEAs to develop policies for meeting the needs of dyslexic children and other children with special needs within their broader educational policies to meet the educational needs of all children. We cite examples of two LEAs where we consider that very positive steps have been taken in this direction over a number of years. Moreover, such policies stand or fall by how they are implemented in individual schools and although, again we were able to identify schools where excellent whole school policies were in operation, we also found variability between schools within LEAs. Even within individual schools there was evidence of variations between the responses of specific teachers to expressed parental concerns and pupil behaviour. The key point to be emphasised here is that whilst first class training and assessment policies at LEA level, complemented by effective teaching and assessment policies in schools, are vitally important for meeting children's needs, it is at the face to face level of interaction between teachers and children, and teachers and parents that the success or failure of such policies depends.

The final **Chapter eight** provides further discussion of the issues highlighted here and offers several conclusions as to possible ways forward.

Main Conclusions and Recommendations

1 **Gap in research**
Our review of the literature shows a gap in research into the parents' perspective on parent professional relationships in the SEN field.

2 **How to understand parent perspective**
Parental perspectives and actions in finding appropriate educational provision for their children were understood in terms of their *strategies* to achieve this end and the way they escalated these strategies, how their efforts were guided by their changing *knowledge* about literacy difficulties and dyslexia and their developing *identities* as parents of a child with dyslexia.

3 **When parents escalate their efforts**
Parents tended to escalate their strategies to secure appropriate provision when two conditions occurred:
(i) Professionals' inappropriate responses: professionals responded to their concerns as an overreaction about their child's learning difficulty or they ignored the parents' concerns, saying that things would come right; and
(ii) the parents' had growing concerns about their child's emotional well being deteriorating.

4 **Parent concerns go beyond dyslexia**
Parents' concerns in the case analyses did not all fit exclusively into broad categories like dyslexia/specific literacy difficulties. The findings, consistent with existing knowledge about the field, show the extent to which dyslexic difficulties are sometimes found to be associated with attentional, hyperactive and emotional and behavioural difficulties, dyspraxic difficulties and, autism.

5 **Focus of development officer's work**
The development officer's work involved more cases where children were receiving additional provision at School Action and School Action plus than at statements levels. This suggests that this kind of development work might be useful to prevent the need for statements to provide additional provision.

6 **Development officer's role like Parent Partnership Officers**
The development officer's role was similar to that specified in the SEN Code of Practice for Parent Partnership Officer – namely, information, publicity, training, advice and support, networking and collaboration.

7 **Value of development officer's work**
Parents supported by the officer valued her independence from the LEAs, her ability to provide

intensive and continuing support and how her presence in meetings provided added pressure for professionals to take them seriously. This independence would be the distinctive feature of parent partnership work funded by an independent voluntary organisation. However, independent parent support work may be better organised to go beyond dyslexia as a single area of learning difficulty as the most complex cases in the project did not fit simple categories of SEN.

8 **Evidence of professionals not practising effective communication**
Evidence from our case studies indicate that professional practice is in general not keeping to the principles of effective communications with parents, set out in the SEN Code of Practice. Linking these findings to other relevant research suggests that our findings have some wider applicability beyond the project sample.

9 **Limits of effective communication in resolving differences**
The study highlights the different views of parents and professionals, for example, what causes literacy difficulties and appropriate educational responses to them. Communications can be difficult when professionals cannot acknowledge parents' knowledge about their child. The study shows differences between parents and professionals over early identification of difficulties in literacy learning, the professional fear of labelling and their dismissal of parents' concerns.

10 **Tension between parent partnership and statement system**
The study highlights the uneasy relationship between partnership principles and the SEN framework whereby parents have recourse to statements in a potentially adversarial system.

11 **Confusion and issues with partnership model**
The study shows confusion over the terms 'participation' and 'partnership'; as to how much professional control is

involved. It also points to practical issues: partnership involves parents and teachers working together, and this requires time and funds which are not always available. Also, the partnership model is not favoured by everyone.

12 Need to see parent-professional relationships in wider social context:
The study indicates that finding ways of establishing constructive communications and partnerships involves taking a wider view of the social and education system. Parent partnership in relation to dyslexia is part of wider and general issues about home-school relations for all children.

13 The importance of extended professionalism
The study indicates the importance of supporting the further development of extended professionalism in this field, that is, sensitivity to parents' perspectives, respect for them and their concerns and interest in their children's education. We argue that extended professionalism needs to become inclusive: it cannot apply to specific areas, like dyslexia, without links to SEN overall and to all children in the general school system.

We recommend that this principle of extended professionalism in relation to parents be used as a criterion for all school and LEA developments as well as in initial and continuing professional development of professionals in the education system.

14 Review and develop dyslexia friendly school concept
We recommend that developments towards making schools more dyslexia friendly be embedded in wider developments of SEN friendly or inclusive schools and general inclusive schools.

15 LEA and school developments
We recommend the wider use of LEA policies that focus on provision for pupils with dyslexic difficulties be interconnected with wider SEN and educational

provision, along the lines of two of the LEAs participating in the study. These cover levels of skills in fields relevant to teachers, SENCOs, and specialist support professionals, focus on early intervention and prevention, use of evidence based teaching and support interventions and a recognition of a continuum of provision from mainstream to specialist centres.

We also recommend the development of LEA systems of allocating additional resources without statements as practised in some of the participant LEAs and recommended recently by the Audit Commission.

16 **Central role of individuals in fostering parent partnership**
The study highlights repeatedly that despite the best systems and policies, in the end good practice depends on the key role of individuals in fostering positive parent-teacher relationships.

Access Arrangements in Examinations

Lynn Greenwold, Chief Executive, Patoss

This article aims to give a brief overview of the principles behind access arrangements in examinations formerly known as special arrangements. Detailed guidance is available from the Joint Council for Qualifications and Patoss – see details at the end of this article. Access arrangements are for students who are significantly disadvantaged by their learning difficulties or physical impairments. When the normal arrangements for assessment present barriers to their showing their true level of competence, other access arrangements might be available, as long as these arrangements do not affect the validity of the assessment. In other words they cannot affect the assessment criteria of the examination or in any other way invalidate what is being assessed.

Some years ago, in the interests of widening access to qualifications, the awarding bodies began granting access arrangements in examinations to candidates with special educational needs. The principles underlying the access arrangements are to carry out examinations that are fair to all candidates with special educational needs while still maintaining the integrity of the examination.

It is important to understand a bit about the principles behind both national qualifications and the examination process to appreciate how these access arrangements can be applied.

The purpose of qualifications is to establish a national standard, in that subject, or area for what the student knows, understands and can do. For any future college, university or prospective employer, a certificate for that qualification is confirmation of what that individual can do. For each qualification there are certain specific requirements that must be met. These are the assessment criteria, i.e. what the assessment is testing.

However, there are some students, who cope well with the learning demands of their course, but for whom the standard arrangements for the assessment of their knowledge and skills present an unnecessary barrier which could be removed without affecting the validity of the assessment. In these instances adjustments can be made to the examination arrangements to permit the student to show their knowledge and skills. For example, if the paper were English Language or English Literature aiming to test a student's reading of English, then clearly having someone to read the paper for her/him would not show that they could do this independently. On the other hand, if the same student were taking History, and were eligible for reading help, s/he would be able to have a reader in this examination, since the examination is testing for knowledge and understanding of History, not for reading skill. It must be stressed that these access arrangements are adjustments, not concessions. The credibility of the qualification must be maintained and have the same value for the disabled person as for any other.

How would a student be considered for access arrangements?

Each student is an individual and has to be considered individually

The Examination Centre, e.g. school or college, must take the lead in deciding this. The process of exploring and applying for access arrangements in examinations is one of co-ordination and co-operation. The examinations officer, SENCo, specialist teacher, assessor and subject teacher all have a role to play in this process and work together as a team. They will know the requirements of the course. These will be considered alongside the requirements of the candidate and implications for assessment at the outset of a course. The requirements of each student are considered individually and may vary for different courses. The information they gather will, where required, be used to inform Awarding Bodies in making their determination of what access arrangements are appropriate. If parents are concerned their son or daughter might require an access arrangement they should contact the examinations officer at the school or college well in advance of the examinations occurring.

The centre will have to consider that they have chosen the most appropriate course for the student and the most appropriate arrangement. They would take account of any special educational needs they are aware of and the student's normal way of working. Some students with specific learning difficulties may not need, or qualify for, the same access arrangements for all examination papers. The student's need for access arrangements must be related to specific examination papers and/or other forms of assessment.

Access arrangements are made to enable the student to demonstrate the knowledge, understanding and skills they have achieved during the course. The arrangements must not give unfair advantage over other candidates. But they are there to remove barriers. They must reflect the student's normal way of working in the classroom and for internal examinations. And they must keep the integrity of the assessment. It should be remembered they are testing the student's knowledge, understanding and skills and the application of these in assessment.

Access arrangements are granted by Awarding Bodies, based on information received from the examinations officer at the centre (the student's school or college). The centre assesses the current needs of the student based on one of the following:

a) A Statement of Special Educational Needs relating to secondary education;

b) A psychological assessment confirming a learning disability, carried out during the secondary school period, by a qualified psychologist confirming a learning disability; or

c) An assessment confirming a learning disability, carried out during the secondary school period, by a specialist teacher holding a JCQ approved qualification.

These decisions are also supported by information from the subject teacher and evidence about the student's normal way of working. Whatever access arrangement is granted, the student must have experience and practice in using it prior to the examination.

What types of access arrangements are there?

There are many types of access arrangement. The most appropriate will be a matter for each individual. The following is a table listing some of those available for general qualifications.

Determined by Centres	Determined by Awarding Bodies
• Up to 25% extra time	• More than 25% extra time
• Supervised rest breaks	• Readers
• Photocopy onto coloured paper	• Scribes
• Coloured overlays	• Practical Assistants
• Transcript	• Word Processors
• Prompters	• Voice-activated computer

National examinations are overseen by the Joint Council for Qualifications, the organisation which represents major awarding bodies in England, Wales and Northern Ireland. These are:

- AQA
- CCEA
- City & Guilds
- Edexcel
- OCR and
- WJEC.

The Joint Council amends the regulations and guidance[1] each year to continue to develop best practice. The Council serves to help public understanding of the work of those groups overseeing and awarding national qualifications.

The Joint Council and the awarding bodies have welcomed comments from Patoss and other professional groups. They have often incorporated these into their guidance and procedures. This autumn has seen a major rewriting of the regulations and guidance. The presentation is much clearer and many of the difficulties dyslexic students have faced in the past are well addressed. The guidance for 2004–05 covers not only GCSE, GCE but also Key Skills and Entry Level qualifications.

The latest guidance encourages forward planning for all students' assessments. In this vein the students should be assessed at the beginning of their course so that applications for arrangements can be made to cover all aspects of submitted work: modules, coursework and examination papers.

Amendments to the regulations for 2004–05, among other points, include use of readers for those for whom not only reading accuracy, and reading speed but also reading comprehension is considered. And clear guidelines are given for determining eligibility.

The Joint Council has continued to confer and work with a range of professionals (including the BDA) to provide the best opportunities for our students to demonstrate their true levels of knowledge, understanding and skills through the formal examinations process. We welcome this continuing partnership.

Sources of more information

Joint Council for Qualifications
Veritas House, Finsbury Pavement, London EC2A 1NQ,
Tel: 020 7638 4125 125
Website: www.jcq.org.uk

Patoss, PO Box 10 Evesham, Worcestershire WR11 1ZQ,
Tel: 01386-712650
Website: www.patoss-dyslexia.org
Email: patoss@evesham.ac.uk

BDA Website: www.bda-dyslexia.org.uk

References

Providing for Candidates with Special Assessment Needs by Gill Backhouse, Patoss, 2000 (updated annually)

Regulations and Guidance for Candidates who are Eligible for Adjustments in Examinations – 1 September 2004 – 31 August 2005; GCE, VCE, GCSE & GNVQ, available from the Joint Council Website: www.jcq.org.uk

New Guidelines for Assessment of Dyslexia in Higher Education:

The Disabled Students' Allowance (DSA)

Bernadette McLean, Helen Arkell Dyslexia Centre and Dr Chris Singleton, University of Hull

What is the DSA?

Students in Higher Education who have disabilities are entitled to financial help through Disabled Students' Allowances known as DSAs. These are available for full and part time students.

Depending on individual needs, support from the DSA can finance things such as specialist equipment, study skills tuition and photocopying costs.

There are four kinds of financial help:

- Specialist equipment allowance of up to £4,565 for the whole course.

- Non medical helper allowance (up to £11,550 for full time study; up to £8,670 for part time study).
- A general disabled student allowance (up to £1,525 for full time study; up to £1,140 for part time study).
- Extra travel costs allowance.

Postgraduate students have one DSA allowance to meet their disability-related course costs, paying up to £5,500.
(figures apply to 2004/05)

How do students get a DSA?

Students should apply to their Local Education Authority (LEA) for advice on making an application for DSA support. The LEA will ask students to have an assessment of their course-related needs at an agreed assessment centre. Such centres are subject to a regular inspection to ensure they meet required standards. The centre will provide a report identifying equipment and any training or non-medical help needed. This is known as a needs assessment.

Further details can be found in *Bridging the Gap: A guide to the Disabled Students Allowances (DSAs) in higher education* which is available from LEAs. More information on help available to students with disabilities can be found on the Skill website. Skill is a national bureau for students with disabilities. www.skill.org.uk.

How does an LEA decide that a needs assessment is warranted?

In order to recommend students for needs assessments LEAs have to decide whether the assessment report that a student offers as "proof" of his disability is acceptable.

What problems have arisen?

Over the past few years the number of DSA applications has soared. It is reckoned that 70% of these applications come from dyslexic students. However, to apply for the DSA, a diagnostic assessment report from a psychologist or other appropriately qualified professional must be produced. There has been uncertainty among those administering DSA applications about what constitutes acceptable evidence for the presence of dyslexia/SpLD. Over the past few years there has also been some confusion over who is eligible to carry out the diagnostic assessment of students. There have been concerns that assessors were not always used to assessing adults and were using diagnostic tools that were inappropriate. In some parts of the country there have been too few professionals to meet the increasing demand for assessment; this has led to delays and students having to wait to receive the support they need for their courses. Furthermore, there have been problems for officials in understanding the reports and determining whether the evidence is conclusive.

The Working Party

In 2003, in response to requests for clarification from LEAs, the Department for Education and Skills (DfES) convened a special working group to revise guidelines on diagnostic assessment of university students with specific learning difficulties (SpLD), including dyslexia, dyscalculia, dyspraxia (developmental co-ordination disorder), and attention deficit disorders.

The DfES co-ordinated the work of the group and hosted the meetings. The group, which is chaired by Carol Youngs, the BDA Policy Director, comprises about 20 professional members, including:

- psychologists;
- disability officers;
- specialist teachers;
- support staff working in HE;

- leaders of training course for teachers of adults with SpLD;
- LEA awards officers; and
- other consultants in relevant fields.

The aims of the working party have been to create a new **National Framework for Assessment of SpLD in Higher Education for Applications for DSA**. In the past there have been many uncertainties amongst LEA officers administering DSA applications because of their limited knowledge of dyslexia and its effects on studying in higher education. These concerns and uncertainties often lead to delays in processing applications and to some students being denied access to the support they require. The new National Framework will:

- provide a fair DSA system that is simple to administer, enabling quicker and easier access for students; and
- establish evidence requirements that LEAs could be confident would provide a reliable professional judgement that a student has SpLD.

This would be achieved by:

- identification of suitable tests and the ongoing updating of such tests for use by appropriately trained and qualified professionals;
- establishing means whereby those with appropriate qualifications are able to obtain and maintain the skills and expertise in administering and interpreting the tests;
- proposing standards and a code of practice for all involved in assessment, including an agreed and accessible format for reports;
- producing clear guidance to LEA awards officers and students to minimise local variances;
- providing advice about identification, assessment and referral of students with any of the named SpLDs namely: dyslexia, dyspraxia, dyscalculia, ADD/ADHD; and

- providing some advice on dealing with complex and borderline cases, including those where English is a second language.

The new Framework, which will be published in 2005 and is expected to take full effect in 2007, will specify which tests should be used, what qualifications and training are required by those carrying out such assessments, and the content and format of reports. The following is a brief outline of the new Framework. For full details please consult the BDA website or the DfES website (www.dfes.gov.uk/studentsupport).

Suitable Tests

The Working Party has drawn up the following principles:

1 Assessment of SpLD requires a range of tests covering general intellectual ability and cognitive processing as well as attainments in literacy and, where appropriate, numeracy

2 Where possible, the tests should be properly standardised on an adult population with clear evidence of validity and reliability

3 The list is consistent with the generally held view that dyslexia is a condition which affects aspects of cognitive functioning, so tests of cognitive functioning are seen as essential for a proper assessment.

4 Supplementary methods of information gathering may be used to inform the diagnostic process. This may be information about conditions such as dyspraxia and attention disorders drawn from observation of the student, assessments by other professionals (e.g. Occupational Therapists) or from the use of recognised checklists.

This list should make authorisation by LEA awards officers more straightforward. Where assessors use alternative tests they should provide a justification for doing so. A panel will review the list periodically and consider new tests for inclusion.

Qualifications and Training of Assessors

The Working Party emphasised that the quality of an assessment and the subsequent report depends mainly on the knowledge and skills of the assessor. Assessments require interpretation of test results and integration of this with other relevant information in order to reach a conclusion. The choice of tests and the results are critical, but they do not tell the whole story.

A key part of the Framework is that those providing assessments for DSA in cases of SpLD by 2007 must hold a Current Practising Certificate in SpLD Assessment. It is expected that all assessors (chartered psychologists, specialist teachers and other qualified professionals) would conform to the standards set out in the Framework. Practising Certificates will have a life of five years and be updated thereafter, contingent upon the assessor having participated in appropriate Continuing Professional Development.

Courses meeting the Assessment Awards and Practising Certificate standards at Level 5 will be accredited through a board coordinated by PATOSS and the BDA. Existing Diploma level training should be suitable with relatively small changes to ensure a minimum of input on psychometric testing principles and practice and more extensive practical experience of assessing adults.

Those currently carrying out assessments will be able to apply for immediate recognition by providing evidence of their competencies, qualifications and experience.

Format for Diagnostic Assessment Reports

Diagnostic assessment reports should present evidence for SpLD to facilitate their perusal by LEA Awards Officers. The information they contain and their format should be as consistent as possible. Essential information needs be given so that the decision that the student has SpLD is clearly based on satisfactory evidence.

The full report of the Working Party was published on the DfES website in July 2004 (see web address below). There was a consultation period until the end of October 2004 and the new Framework will be contained in DfES guidance to LEAs, given in February 2005.

References

For further information about Disabled Students Allowances see:

- www.bda-dyslexia.org.uk/main/information/adults/a07dsa.asp.
- www.dyslexic.com/database/articles/dsa.html.

For further information about the report of the Working Party see:

- www.dfes.gov.uk/studentsupport/dsa_1.shtml.
- www.bda-dyslexia.org.uk.

Chris Singleton can be contacted at C.Singleton@hull.ac.uk

Index of Acronyms

DSA	Disabled Students' Allowance
LEA	Local Education Authority
EP	Educational Psychologist
SpLD	Specific Learning Difficulty/Difficulties

ADD	Attention Deficit Disorder
ADHD	Attention Deficit Disorder with Hyperactivity
HE	Higher Education
DfES	Department for Education and Skills
PATOSS	Professional Association of Teachers of Students with SpLD

Part 5

ICT

This CAP can fit dyslexic children!

Jeff Hughes

When the Communication Aids Project (CAP) was first discussed it was not entirely clear whether many children with dyslexia and other specific learning difficulties would be able to benefit. This £10 million pot of additional funding was intended to provide communications aids which would be used by the child as they progressed through the education system and would not be snatched back because they changed school.

Chris Stevens and Mick Thomas of BECTA (the British Educational Communications Technology Association) were adamant that they wanted the project to support all children who had a difficulty in communication. They had the vision to see that well chosen ICT resources could make a big difference to dyslexic children. So by the time CAP was launched in April 2002, Ability Net had joined the project to lead the assessment of children with dyslexia.

This first phase of this truly multi-agency project, which draws together education, health, social services and the voluntary sector, trained a band of local assessors. These specialists would be charged with making sure that children, having had their needs properly identified, would be well supported so they could use their equipment effectively.

Soon there was such a demand that the original pot of money ran out well before the end of the project's planned two year life. This prompted the Department for Education and Skills, which had funded the first phase of the project, into providing a second phase over two more years from 2004 to 2006. Plans were also put into place for how the project's objectives would be continued beyond 2006.

Examples of dyslexic children helped range from those who cannot work in handwriting and need the support of a simple portable word processor, to those who need a word processor with dyslexia aware spell checking, to those who need to have documents scanned in so they can be read by the computer, to those who cannot type effectively and need to dictate to their computer and have it type their words for them.

To find out more go and look at the CAP web site at http://cap.becta.org.uk

The procedure for getting resources is quite simple and referral is made using forms available on the CAP website. An application can be made by anyone concerned with the education of the child including a parent, carer or guardian, a teacher or a therapist. The criteria for getting support are quite strict and the project will not pay for equipment if this could undermine the school or LEA legal duty to provide for the child! For many dyslexic children, filling in the form has proven to be well worth the effort, and the project should be helping many, many more in the future!

Edington & Shapwick School

This is a pioneering Independent school of proven reputation, set close to historic Glastonbury and specialising in educating dyslexic children aged eight to eighteen years.

We understand the importance of creating that vital atmosphere of confidence and self-esteem without which dyslexic youngsters cannot reach true potential.

One in ten children is known to experience a significant degree of dyslexic handicap. Mainstream education fails them. Independent schooling, however prestigious, fares little better with its system of specialist streaming or extraction.

Those who experience dyslexia's cruel handicaps need the understanding of fellow pupils who share their difficulties and the guidance of teachers who have dedicated themselves and the whole curriculum to special needs.

We provide a highly personalised teacher – pupil ratio of one to eight.

- A very broad curriculum typical of a much larger school, incorporating ICT across the curriculum to GCSE and AL.
- A full programme of sport, games and fixtures, visits and residential trips.
- Wide ranging extra curricular activities. A well qualified staff who have won the warmest praise from OFSTED Inspectors.
- CreSTed Category 'A' School.

Come and meet us.

Boys and Girls aged 8 to 13 years
Telephone: 01278 722012
Email:
edington@edingtonshapwick.co.uk

Boys and Girls aged 13 to 18 years
Telephone: 01458 210384
Email:
shapwick@edingtonshapwick.co.uk

Website: www.edingtonshapwick.co.uk

Study Skills and ICT

Ian Smythe and EA Draffan

Study skills may be thought of as those skills over and above reading and writing that are necessary to help demonstrate ones potential in a given area. They can apply it to coursework, examinations or at work. It would be easy to list all the technology that one could use. However, since that information can be found elsewhere, let us look at some of the issues, including advantages and disadvantages, and some of the tricks of how to use technology successfully.

Asking the right questions (and time management)

Do you ever wonder where the hours have gone, and why there is no time to do anything? Try this website: www.ucc.vt.edu/stdysk/TMInteractive.html.

It is not specific to students, but will help the reader understand what can happen when there is no time management in place. Time can disappear when you least expect it! No level of electronic sophistication will help if you don't train yourself (or forget) to put in the "appointments"! Conversely, if you don't check it, or miss the alarm, then the device is useless.

The starting point for time management when choosing technology should be to ask *"What do I need to remember?"*

After that comes *"Can I train myself to use it?"* and *"What happens when I lose it?"*

Then there are questions such as "*What other information do I need to store?*" and "*What about 'technology synchronisation?*".

That is, if you have a handheld device and a computer based diary, you need to be sure they say the same thing! "*Do I need to transfer information from a device to the computer?*"

(Note that although these comments are written for the reader, the principles hold true if you are buying for a child.)

Then you must consider how the device will remind you:
"Do I need to check it, or is there an alarm?"
"Will I always have the device with me, or is there a chance that I will miss the alarm?" "What happens when the alarm goes off when I am doing something else – will it sound again in 15 minutes, or just hope that I will remember?"

Then there is the question of portability.

"Do I need reminders at all times of the day (and therefore need a handheld device), or is just a morning reminder good enough (when a home based computer would suffice)".

Interestingly, in this age when we have so many electronic alternatives, many individuals have gone back to a paper based diary or Filofax. Many prefer the physical side, such as seeing coloured markers sticking out, and flicking or spreading out pages.

And the trick? The trick is not to assume there is a perfect device to remind you of everything. The trick is to enter all the appointments, to back up, and not rely on any single device!

Deciding what you are trying to do (and taking notes)

Taking notes can be a problem. Whether it is in GCSE Chemistry, or university courses on Tectonic Plates, the principles are the same. Information is being delivered verbally along with some visuals. How does one capture that information so that it may be reproduced in some examination in future. There are several ways, some of which have technology solutions. The problem is to find the right answer for a given individual.

The main recording methods are:

- handwritten notes;
- concept and mindmapping the lecture;
- sound recording; and
- typing directly into computer.

Each has advantages and disadvantages. Handwritten notes are low tech, and great if you can write fast enough, and at a later date read and understand what you have written! Concept maps can be useful if you can get down enough information. The lecture usually has a logical structure, and so it is relatively easy to create the concept map. Sound recording is good, as you can record easily and listen later. But it assumes that the sound quality will be good enough. If you need to transcribe it into notes, that can be laborious.

Typing directly onto a laptop computer is another alternative. But who can type fast enough while they are trying to understand and synthesise the content. How many dyslexic individuals are given typing courses when they are given computers? However, despite disability legislation (e.g. DDA Part 4), few classrooms and lecture theatres offer convenient power sockets, and if you need to work for more than a couple of hours, this is a real problem. Whatever method is used, the important part is how it forms part of the course notes, and how they are used to help the revision process.

And the trick? The trick is not to assume that technology can help solve the problems. The trick is to ask what are the problems, and find the best solutions!

Technology Overkill (and reading and writing)

There are many technologies that can support reading and writing skills from computer based software (spellcheckers with speech, text-to-speech software, grammar checkers, word predictors etc.) to the hand-held pocket dictionaries. But again it is important to consider what you really want to do.

Consider the talking word processor EdWord, developed by the University of Manchester Institute of Science and Technology, that can be downloaded for free (www.deafblindonline.org.uk). It offers just seven options (five under File and two under Format), and yet you can do just about everything, such as:

- change background and font colours (easier than in Word!);
- saving the file;
- have the text read to you; and
- copy and paste items from other places and have them read aloud.

The software becomes more hassle free and dyslexia friendly by being simplified. The point is that often the technology is over complicated, (we reckon we have used only about 10% of the 227 items that appear in the drop down menus of our versions of Microsoft Word!) Do not assume increased functionality will increase the ability or speed the writing process. Often it just adds to the confusion.

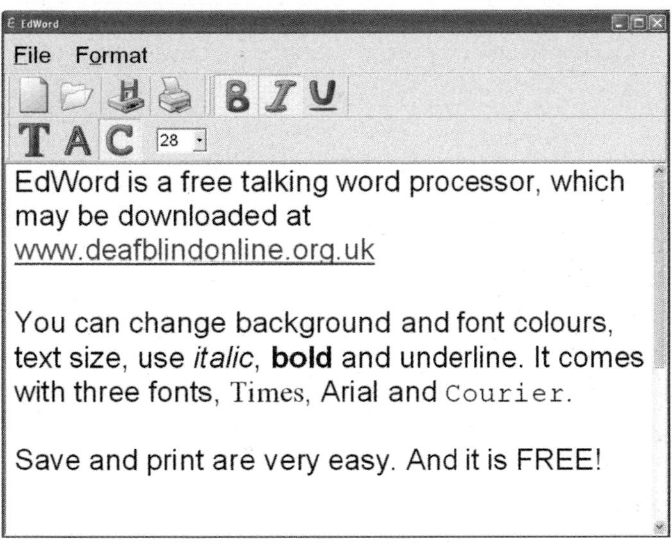

A screen shot of "EdWord"

Spellcheckers

Just how good are spell checkers? When you make a mistake, how do you know which is the right word? Does word prediction work in a way that is useful to you? And why does a grammar checker keep coming up with errors for perfectly good English? It is trying to confuse us?

And the trick? The trick is not to buy software that could do everything. The trick is buy a tool that does what you want it to do, and master those skills perfectly!

Using shorthand (and planning and concept mapping)

It does not matter if you are planning an assignment for school or developing a thesis for university, unless there is structure to what you submit, the content will

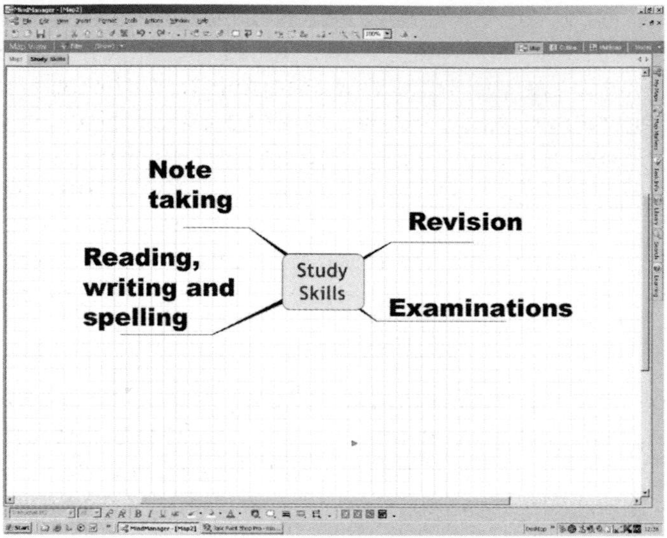

Mindmanager example

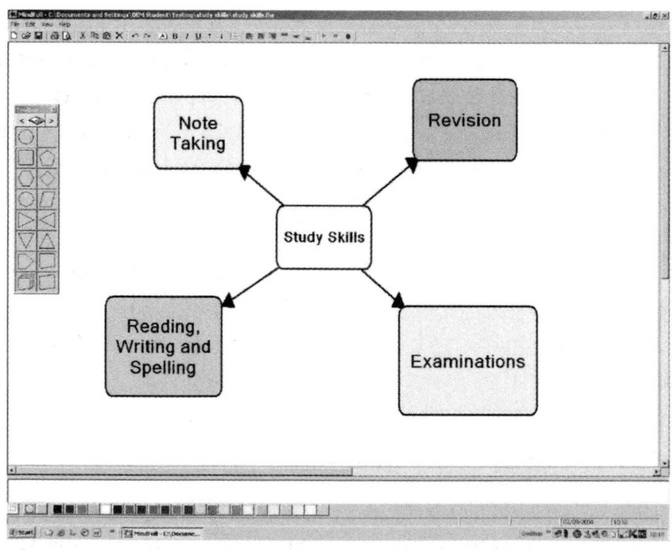

MindFull example

be incoherent, and you will lose marks. One of the most useful tools for the dyslexic individual is concept mapping (sometimes referred to as mindmapping). Although paper versions are very easy, many prefer to use electronic versions, particularly as they are easy to modify, and can hide earlier "adjustments". Research suggests that 70% of dyslexics use just one type of concept mapping tool – Inspiration. But there are a number of tools out there that can do the job, and they all have different abilities and methods of presentation.

In some concept mapping packages, presentation style can be changed. But all too frequently individuals end up with the style that is the default, or the style of the person that taught them how to use it (if anybody did!). When we look at the software, how many people use all the functions? Do you need those "voice notes"? Do you want an extensive library of images? Do you want to draw your own images? Only by looking at the alternatives can you decide what works best for you. Some find that the computer version is too cumbersome, and revert to paper versions. Others try it, and decide concept mapping is not for them. But most dyslexic individuals find the method helps to clarify thoughts and create a foundation to build upon. However, it is rare that the concept map is the piece of work that may be submitted for marking.

And the trick? The trick is not to make an extensive concept/mindmap that have extensive branches. The trick is to develop the ability to turn a concise concept/mindmap into an essay!

The Failsafe (and examinations)

One of the biggest problems with technology is that when it is needed most (such as in examinations) you may not be able to use your specially adapted programs which suit your specific needs, e.g. modified spellcheckers. Although times are changing, as are the regulations, the use of technology still does not keep pace with policies (e.g. the Code of Practice and DDA Part 4) that states that the examination should assess ability and not disability, and that the individual should not be disadvantaged in an examination due to their disability. How can it be fair to allow the technology aids on a daily basis, and then exclude their adaptations and modifications in the exam? What do the examiners think is the purpose of the exam? What is really being tested?

And the trick? The trick is not to have plenty of batteries (though it helps). The trick is practice what to do when (not if) the technology fails!

Conclusions

When it comes to technology, there is no universal solution. Some technology can help, but having more money to buy more expensive "solutions" will not make much difference. What will make a difference is training: training in how to understand the needs, training in how to understand the technology and how to use it, and training in how to convert what the technology offers into better outcomes for life as well as results for examinations. We should not attempt to hold out for better technologies, because it will not be coming in the near future. Unfortunately the technologies may become so central to working that the anxiety of having them creates more problems than the actual difficulties of not having them. The answer is to ask what is required to improve study skills and then seek appropriate solutions, some of which may include information and communication technology (ICT).

References

To avoid having to retype long web addresses, a dedicated website has been created to accompany this article. It may be found at: www.emptech.info/bda2004studyskills.html

Using Speech Recognition Software

Malcolm Litten, Mark College

I cannot recall speaking to any teacher who said it would be wrong to use speech recognition software (SRS) with a dyslexic pupil. It seems everyone accepts that in theory this would be a boon for many of their pupils. But in practice it is still all too rarely offered.

Some research into its value for pupils experiencing severe difficulties with written expression illustrated why this might be so. The research aimed to measure whether there was increased speed of output compared with typing, and to compare the accuracy of output in both modes. While most pupils in the small study increased their speed of output significantly, none achieved a high level of accuracy. The study concluded that the software posed the users many problems.

This conclusion was reasonable – but only in the peculiar circumstances in which SRS was evaluated. The pupils had been given a single session of training in its use. In a similar study with undergraduates reported in *Dyslexia* a little while ago, <u>no</u> training was provided. Unsurprisingly, the conclusions were again negative. Given the same level of training, we would all conclude that the car was a lethal tool that should never be given to young people. Too often, conclusions about SRS have been dismissive because expectations of it have been so unreasonable. When teachers and educational psychologists widely recommend the use of a word processor (and, by implication, of a keyboard) to help many dyslexics with their writing and spelling, the expectations do not usually include that the user must be a highly proficient touch-typist, simply that typing skills may need to be developed. Many users benefit substantially from the use of a word processor and a spell checker without becoming very rapid or accurate typists. Is it that the producers of SRS have oversold their product while understating the need for training? Almost certainly this is the case. But I also think we have too narrow and mechanical a basis for evaluation, so I would like to suggest a wider one.

While speed and accuracy of production are entirely valid and relevant measures of success, there are many others, for example, readability. If written output is often unreadable (through the bizarre nature of the spelling rather than just the handwriting) then SRS will transform this – provided, of course, that the words on the page are the intended ones. Achieving this is just the kind of problem so often reported. But the solutions are available: in addition to adequate training, which is essential, coupling SRS with *Keystone ScreenReader* can provide essential feedback on accuracy if the user's own reading is not adequate.

What about quantity of output? Many dyslexic pupils I work with can, when discussing a topic, produce extensive responses but the consequent piece of writing produced by conventional means is very short. Capturing what the pupil can *say* can transform output.

If a pupil has rarely written at any appreciable length, SRS can, for the first time, open up the opportunity for pupil and teacher to address the many challenges of extensive writing for the first time. At its simplest, it is impossible to discuss the use of paragraphs if the entire piece is rarely longer than three or four sentences.

A similar story can emerge over the quality of expression. Written expression is often compromised by the difficulty of spelling more elaborate, adventurous vocabulary, so plain simple words are used instead. SRS is actually better with 'difficult' words because it has more information to go on.

When it comes to producing written work, the self confidence of many dyslexics can be extremely low. Confidence in general in the educational setting can improve with successful use of SRS.

Dependence on others can develop in an unhelpful way with some dyslexic pupils. One of the significant benefits I have seen from the use of SRS is far greater independence.

Benefits in any of these aspects may be significant steps forward. Over time, they may quite possibly also lead to a reduced need for SRS. There are certainly examples of improvement in the more traditional forms of written expression as a result of success with SRS.

If the expectation, or even the requirement, is perfection in accurate output, then SRS is not and never will be good enough. However, by any reasonable assessment of success, it is now far better than just "good enough". Of all the many ways in which computer technology helps dyslexics, in my experience SRS has produced the most transforming consequences. If there were just one pupil in every school in the UK who would be helped by being offered SRS, that represents thousands of children who *should* be given that chance.

The practical considerations

There is a general consensus that *Dragon* SRS is the best available. It comes in two versions – discrete and continuous. While the continuous version, *Dragon NaturallySpeaking*, is the up-to-date software and so in many ways superior, the discrete version, *DragonDictate*, should not be dismissed out of hand. For some, the more measured pace of delivery can be positively helpful and it remains the easier version to manage corrections in, particularly with the assistance of *Keystone ScreenReader.*

Training is essential. In practice, this has meant about 2–3 hours of one-to-one training, followed by the availability of help if needed. This training should take place over a few days, allowing plenty of opportunity for reinforcement of skills. The intention should be that practical management of the software becomes automatic (just like driving) so that attention is focused on the content of the writing.

I have mentioned *Keystone ScreenReader* more than once. It has been separately developed for dyslexic users of *Dragon* products and offers immediate text-to-speech feedback of everything that appears on screen, and significant help with the reading in the initial training session. Other features offer help with homophones and with spelling.

The necessary computer specifications vary with the two different version of *Dragon. Dragon NaturallySpeaking* requires a powerful processor such as a Pentium 4 and at least 256 Mb of RAM (512 Mb for choice.) In contrast, *DragonDictate* will only require a Pentium chip or better and 64 Mb of RAM. Both require a good quality duplex soundcard – standard in nearly all recent computers. Once again, the software producers let themselves down by providing inferior headsets with their product. As the link between user and computer, quality of headset is vital. Good quality headsets, such as a Plantronics Stereo headset, cost around £25.

IT Help for the Workplace

Ian Litterick, Abi James, Julian Young, iANSYST Limited

Dyslexia is likely to be one of the most common disabilities affecting your employees. According to the British Dyslexia Association (BDA) around 10% of people are dyslexic with about 4% (one in twenty-five) severely affected. Dyslexic employees have different difficulties and some often surprisingly useful abilities to match. The most common outcomes for dyslexia are: difficulty with reading, writing and learning; difficulty remembering; structuring and organising; and reading maps.

In the workplace this can lead to problems with written communication with colleagues and other stakeholders; organising work; reading instructions and maps.

The benefits of dyslexia

On the plus side, dyslexic people often have strengths in seeing the overall picture, in solving problems quickly and in visual skills. However, their difficulties can lead to unemployment or underemployment. By becoming a dyslexia-friendly workplace you can tap into a large underutilised resource.

There is much that employers can do to make the work environment easier for dyslexic employees. The BDA have detailed guidelines for being a dyslexia friendly employer. For example, it is good policy to make sure that all your literature, internal as well as external, electronic as well as paper based, is in plain English and dyslexia friendly. The BDA also have good guidelines on presentation which are available on their website. Many aspects of these will benefit your non dyslexic staff; and improve your communication with customers (remembering that a good few of them are likely to dyslexic too). It will be worth following the guidelines in:

- recruitment policies and procedures;
- literature;
- reviews and appraisals;
- training;
- personnel and support.

One other thing to consider to make your organisation disability and dyslexia friendly is having a website and intranet that are accessible to people with reading impairments. The Office of the e-Envoy has a set of Guidelines for UK government websites http://e-government.cabinetoffice.gov.uk/Resources/WebGuidelines/fs/en which are excellent for any organisation aiming to satisfy the DDA. You can also use Texthelp's BrowseAloud, www.browsealoud.com so that people can listen to your web site, as well as read it.

There's a carrot. It is good policy to do so, and you will be maximising your use of your staff. But there is a stick too: The Disability Discrimination Act 1995 is now in force and will be used by employees who believe that they are being discriminated against because of their dyslexia. And because dyslexia is a 'hidden disability' you may not be aware which of your staff are dyslexic – and the act still applies to them even if they have not declared their dyslexia.

Access to work

The DDA says that you must make "reasonable adjustments". This will often include technological support – computer, specialist software and other electronic aids and gadgets. In many cases in the UK you will be able to get financial support from the Department for Work and Pensions' (Jobcentre Plus) Access to Work scheme for the adjustments that you make for dyslexic staff. See www.dyslexic.com/grants.

This process takes a little time, but the person gets a proper assessment of their strengths and weaknesses and recommendations of specific adjustments, including technology, that will help overcome the difficulties. This will usually produce much better results than a few ad hoc adjustments.

The technology assessment may recommend a variety of tools depending on the person's job and their needs. A computer: on their own, editing and spellchecking can make a huge difference to the ability to write. A laptop is often appropriate so that notes can be taken anywhere and work done at home or whilst travelling. Even with the help of technology dyslexic people will usually need longer to produce the same amount of written material. And many find producing good work in a busy open-plan office next to impossible.

The technology

This section looks at some of the most popular and practical solutions for overcoming difficulties associated with dyslexia in the workplace. For further information visit the web version of this article at www.dyslexic.com/employers which includes web links.

Turning text into speech

For proofreading and for reading text on the computer use text-to-speech software. Add a scanner and optical character recognition software (OCR) for converting print into an electronic version that you can listen to. **Texthelp Read & Write Gold** is the classic tool for dyslexia. It includes text-to-speech and OCR. It also has a dyslexia specific phonetic spell checker, word prediction, help with homophones, thesaurus, dictionary, research and web search tools.

Dictating into your computer

Speech recognition software can be easier than typing and makes spelling mistakes a thing of the past. With training and practice text can be composed quicker than typing. The current market-leader is **Dragon NaturallySpeaking v8**. The **Preferred** version is aimed at small-business and is fine if you only want to use it with Microsoft Office but if you want to dictate into other applications such as contact managers or bespoke applications you will need the **Professional** version which includes macro tools for using Dragon with virtually any program. But there are issues to do with using speech recognition – particularly privacy, composing and proofreading – which mean that speech recognition is not an automatic panacea. With a portable digital recorder, such as the **Olympus DM-20,** you can dictate away from your computer and then transcribe it through Dragon later.

Concept mapping software to help with organising ideas and written work

Concept mapping software allows you to use your visual skills:

- to organise existing knowledge and ideas;
- to plan new writing and projects.

Software packages such as **MindGenius** or **Mind Manager** have been designed as business tools and can used for planning and creating presentations, brain storming, report and project planning.

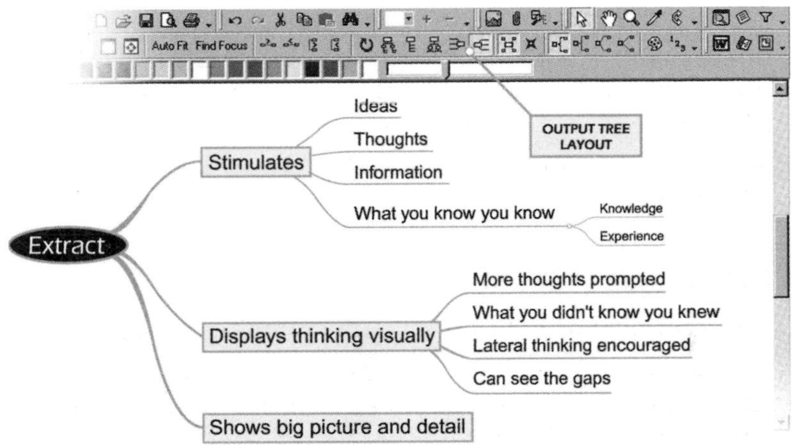

PDA for organising time and remembering things

Time management and organisation can be as much an issue as literacy in the workplace, particularly if your job involves working in different locations, travelling a lot or being away from a computer. Personal Digital Assistants or PDAs running the Palm or Pocket PC operating systems provide pocket-sized devices with many tools including:

- calendar with alarm function;
- to-do list;
- contact list;
- memo pad;
- word processor and spreadsheet applications.

They can also be used to take notes by adding a folding keyboard and there are literally thousands of applications available for them from specialist dictionaries to concept mapping programs. Many mobile phones now come with similar organisational tools and have the added bonus of being able to download emails or access the internet while on the move.

If you find using a stylus or the small screen too inhibiting then an alternative is the AlphaSmart Dana. This combines a full-size keyboard with the Palm operating system giving a light, but robust laptop alternative. Concept mapping and text-to-speech applications are available for the Dana.

Recorder/dictating machine for recording notes and memos

These small devices can record discussions so that you can refer to them later – ideal if you find it difficult to take notes during meetings. You can also use them with speech recognition software to transcribe your own voice notes. Some digital recorders, such as the **Olympus DM-1** and **DM-20**, also store MP3 or other audio files. So you can listen to audio books or recordings of your documents (which you can create with Read & Write Gold) while on the go. If you find that you forget information quickly then you may find a voice memo useful. These can record short messages and most mobile phones or PDAs now include this function.

Satellite navigation system for getting to places without getting lost

Many people with dyslexia find it difficult to remember directions or read road signs quickly enough. For jobs that involve a lot of travelling a satellite navigation system, added to an iPAQ PDA (or installed in the car) will give you directions as you drive.

Scanning Pen

These small devices allow you to store printed text, such as business cards, quotes and web links, by running the tip of the pen over the text, and then transfer it directly to the computer. This makes copying errors less likely. The latest model, the **Quicklink Pen Elite**, can also read aloud scanned in sentences to help overcome reading or pronunciation difficulties.

Further information

Join the DisInEmp forum if you have a professional interest in Disability in Employment (including dyslexia). ,It's a source of mutual help for meeting DDA needs: (www.groups.yahoo.com/group/disinemp).

iANSYST's www.dyslexic.com website has more information on all the products mentioned.

Key 4 Learning's http://www.key4learning.com/ Hidden Disabilities Toolkit is a guide to a whole organisation approach to dyslexia. An early version is published on the Cabinet Office's website http://www.diversity-whatworks.gov.uk/Dyslexia_toolkit/index.html;

Peter Rainger's paper A Dyslexic Perspective on e-Content Accessibility explains how dyslexia affects web use and what you can do to make sites easier to use.

iANSYST Ltd specialises in technology to help dyslexic people make the most of their abilities, and runs the website www.dyslexic.com.

The BDA offer dyslexia awareness training in the workplace. For more information see the BDA website at www.bda-dyslexia.org.uk/main/campaigning/bda-training.asp or contact 0118 966 2677/training@bda-dyslexia.demon.co.uk

The ARROW Approach for Dyslexic Learners

Dr Colin Lane

ARROW recording/playback technology was developed during the 1970s for listening and speech skills improvement and required children to compare adult voices with their own. It quickly became apparent that children, when listening to their own voices, showed increased auditory attention, and preference for their voice, the Self-Voice. The link between the recorded Self-Voice and the internalising processes so necessary to learning, became evident when children and adults, without prompting, silently mouthed their recordings on playback. Research during the 1980s confirmed that the child's Self-Voice was liked more than other voices, and was instantly recognised. Later work suggests that word information recall is better achieved when listening to the Self-Voice.

ARROW is an acronym for Aural Read Respond Oral Write. The system requires a student to interact with the Self-Voice through a series of comprehension and dictation processes. The approach gives the student learning independence, whilst additionally involving high repetition of spoken or textual material. The use of the Self-Voice is central to ARROW and the approach itself is appropriate for all ages and abilities of students.

Research and clinical observations show that ARROW helps to improve many learning skills. These include listening to environmental noise sounds, consonant discrimination, sentence understanding, short term memory for words and digits, and vocalisation. Handwriting and self esteem are also reported to improve following ARROW. Many adults with aphasia, brain injury or learning problems have made marked improvements in short term memory tasks in addition to improving their speech, reading and spelling.

Literacy skill improvements

Since 1986, evidence has been gathered showing the effectiveness of ARROW for the improvement of literacy skills. Rapid yet sustained improvements in reading and spelling have been noted. Tutors trained in ARROW include teachers, psychologists, speech and language therapists, teaching assistants and parents. Results show that word attack skills, sentence reading, spelling and listening improvements emerge within a few hours of commencing ARROW. Analysis of the latest results submitted to the ARROW Centre from 72 tutors is most encouraging:

- 609 students worked between 8–10 hours on ARROW.
- The average age was 10.9 years.
- Average standardised reading age before ARROW was 8.6 years realising a performance/age deficit of 2.3 years.
- Average standardised spelling age before ARROW was 8.1 years, realising a performance or age deficit of 2.8 years.
- After 8–10 hours ARROW reading averaged 9 months improvement, an increase of 23.5%.
- Spellings averaged 7 months improvement, an increase of 19.3% across the same time scale.

Long term studies show improvements are maintained across non intervention periods and further progress is made during later interventions.

The ARROW CD-ROM Material

The recently introduced ARROW CD-ROM system is extremely effective. Material shadows the National Literacy Strategy spelling recommendations. Key Stage 1 material includes high and medium frequency words, calendar information, number and common colour words, phonics including short vowels, consonant blends, end consonant clusters and long vowel phonemes. Key Stage 2 material includes medium frequency words. Key Stage 3 material includes plurals, phonemic segmentation, syllabification, antonym prefixes, consonant suffixes, 'shun' suffixes, homophones, analogy, letter strings, unstressed vowels, unsounded consonants, root words and apostrophes of omission. There is an inter-relationship between levels, and students can readily move between these levels using the ARROW format.

Personalised Spelling Profile Programme

ARROW has developed a CD-ROM Personalised Spelling Profile Programme. Assessments establish each student's individual spelling error patterns. The student then meets a series of Self-Voice correction programmes. The student works alone, moving on to each identified programme until all error patterns have been covered. Children from 7 years of age cope with the Personalised Spelling Profile Programme.

Topic Material

Each ARROW CD-ROM contains graded reading ability topics. The differentiated Topics are based upon Towns and Cities, Transport, Nature and Wildlife. The topics require a student to undertake Self-Voice dictation with an option to complete comprehension tasks. Topic material can be customised according to individual needs or learning centre requirements.

The CD-ROM Features

The CD-ROM contains innovative Self-Voice learning features. Text is shown on screen and is linked to movie sequences. This movie facility has proved extremely helpful for speech and language development work. A text typing facility allows a student to type from the Self-Voice and to compare their efforts against the original text. The relationship between poor listening skills and poor literacy skills is well established. An auditory attention feature gives a student practice in listening to their own voice against a selection of background noises.

Tutors using the new system note that their students pay more attention when using the CD-ROM system than the earlier ARROW audio cassette approach. Within two or three minutes instruction time learners are able to operate the system and begin working on their own.

Results using the ARROW CD-ROM

The ARROW CD-ROM was piloted in Somerset with an hourly five-day programme. 20 children aged between 9 and 13 years undertook ARROW. Four of the children in the project had been excluded from normal classroom provision because of behavioural difficulties. All children were given an appropriate level ARROW CD-ROM based on standardised reading and spelling assessments. 10 children worked simultaneously on laptops with minimal supervision. Results after 5 one hour sessions showed a 9 month improvement in word attack skills and a 4 month improvement in spelling.

A school in the West Midlands has recently introduced ARROW. Year 3 – Year 6 children worked on a 20 minute a session basis for 12 sessions using selected material. Results (standardised tests) show an average 11.5 month improvement in reading and a 6.5 month improvement for spelling. The teacher Barbara Tomlinson reports:

> *".... they are organised and self-motivated to get on by themselves. Their confidence and self-esteem has blossomed and so have their results which you can see. We wish there were more hours in the day so that we could involve more children. All these children are special needs children within school, all have IEP's and work with me during the week."*

School age children undertaking CD-ROM distance learning programmes have achieved similar success. Mrs Allyson Howarth, a parent, writes:

> *"... Monica's reading and spelling has shown measurable improvement and more importantly her confidence and fluency in group reading ... "*

Work with Dyslexic Military Personnel

Military establishments have used the new ARROW CD-ROM system. The Royal Commando Training Establishment, Lympstone, introduced ARROW in order to improve a medical orderly's report writing skills. Working independently on customised medical report type material and standard ARROW programmes, the orderly rapidly improved his report writing, reading and spelling skills.

The ARROW Tutor at HM Naval Base Portsmouth is directing help towards ratings with literacy problems. A customised CD-ROM 'The Age of Nelson' is being implemented alongside standard ARROW material. The officer in charge commented that within two weeks of a severely dyslexic rating commencing ARROW there was a "definite improvement" in his literacy skills. The rating himself reported that he found it easiest to listen to his own voice and take dictation whilst accessing text. Speed reading of the rating improved some 200% across a single training session.

In summary, ARROW is of considerable help to dyslexic students of all ages but training for tutors or parents is essential in order to implement the system successfully.

Further details from

The ARROW Centre
Crypton House
Bridgwater College
Bristol Road
Bridgwater TA6 4SY
Email drcolinlane@yahoo.co.uk
www.self-voice.com
Tel/Fax 01278 450932

Making E-learning Dyslexia Friendly

Ian Smythe

The extent to which learning has become computer based has risen considerably over the past three years. With the EU declaring ICT skills as a new basic skill, we can expect this "e-learning" to become the dominant way of learning in the near future. However, the promise of a multimedia interactive method which encourages learning at a distance has not been fulfilled for dyslexic students. But why not? One reason is that the difficulties encountered by dyslexic individuals were either not previously present, or were addressed by the human element of learning. Furthermore, those providing the material – website developers, course content managers or just lecturers uploading their notes and PowerPoint presentations – do not understand the issues. Not only can these issues be easily addressed if basic guidelines are followed, but also they must be addressed to comply with the latest legislation.

There are many articles that attempt to provide guidelines on accessibility of e-learning (see the references at the end of this article for examples). However, few go beyond the superficial level of the ability to use assistive technology. But there is more to being dyslexia friendly than just asking if the text-to-speech software can read what is on the screen.

Case Studies

In order to understand the sorts of problems we are talking about, let us look at some specific examples. Here are some accessed on the web in June 2004.

a) A screen where there are 50 areas that can be "clicked". This creates considerable confusion through excessive choices, confusing labels and minimising the active working area.

b) The vocabulary used in test questions on a NVQ business management course were above university level, sometimes ambiguous, and did not say which responses were wrong and why.

c) Fancy animation that looked exciting offered no additional information. Instead it confused the learner since it was distracting and took concentration away from the subject material. Furthermore, valuable time was lost in trying to establish if the animation did have a purpose.

d) A live chat zone was used for communication with other students and tutors. However, the chat zone did not have a spellchecker. Consequently the message has to be submitted without checking the spelling, or checked in another program (e.g. Microsoft Word) for cutting and pasting, by which time the chat has moved on to another subject. Furthermore, the background and font colours could not be changed, nor the font style.

When looking at developing and choosing e-learning materials, one has to remember that every individual is different. In developing effective e-learning, it is important to consider:

- Accessibility.
- Usability.
- Readability.

- Learnability.
- Human interaction.

Accessibility

This refers to the ability to access the structure and content of the information through the use of relevant assistive technologies such as text-to-speech.

Usability

Usability is the ease of use of the environment within which you learn. Issues that need consideration within usability include:

- Fonts (style and size).
- Colours (backgrounds, fonts, navigation etc).

There is much debate on which colour is the best background, and in an ideal world, if it would be best to choose the colour personally. In an attempt to look at this, there is a poll being carried out at www.dyslexia.com/qaweb.htm to see preferences. At the date of access (June 2004) based on nearly 6500 voters, background colour preferences were as follows:

- 28% prefer white;
- 22% prefer blue; and
- 19% prefer cream.

This appears to contradict the BDA and ADO claim that cream is preferred. However, one cannot assume that all voters were dyslexic, and the website uses a default white background and a pale blue theme which may influence the result. Also the website reports that 50% prefer Arial, and only 29% prefer Times (based on 2000 voters), though Times was used as the default on the web page to explain the information.

Navigation should be consistent and intuitive as well as clear. Unfortunately even those attempting to promote the issues do not understand them. For example, the navigation buttons on the W3 "slide presentation" on accessibility jump around from slide to slide! (www.w3.org/Talks/WAI-Intro/slide1-0.html)

Readability

Text should be age, culture and content appropriate. This means choosing vocabulary according to needs. Keep sentence structure simple, and ensure the content can be understood by all. To check the readability of your material, try looking at www.readability.org.

Learnability

The introduction of computers into mainstream education has provided the potential to present learning in new and exciting ways. This includes not only the role of multimedia, but also the potential for self-learning through exploration. However, many of these ideas are still very new, and not well understood. As a consequence, e-learning is still little more than books with a multimedia component, despite claims to the contrary. E-learning needs to retain a structured, sequential learning style, with a logical progression tailored to individual needs, without limiting the potential for exploration. Few programmes provide an opportunity to switch between pedagogic approaches, and when the approach does change, it is only a sequential change, not a response to failing to learn by offering an alternative one.

Human Interaction

Most individuals, dyslexic and non-dyslexic, report that learning is a better experience when there is some interaction, both with tutors and with fellow students.

Over and above these issues, consideration should be given to examination and coursework which should assess ability and not disability.

Putting it All Together – A Case Study

Dystrain is a pan-European project led by the Welsh Dyslexia Project. It aims to deliver training to teachers and to parents on supporting the dyslexic individual. Many of the learners on the course are dyslexic, and therefore the course has been centred on the needs of the dyslexic individual, knowing that "what is good for dyslexics is good for all" (the slogan of the Adult Dyslexia Organisation). Consequently, the course has developed using good e-learning design principles, including:

- the ability to modify the background colour, and font size and colour;
- one main text area, which can be accessed by screen readers;
- a clearly marked secondary "zone" for additional information, including videos;
- simple consistent navigation, with one main navigation button, one help button and a "dictionary" button;
- a clear interface and a consistent layout across all modules;
- structured sequential learning, using pictures, sound and video;
- human support, through webcams and face-to-face meetings; and
- examinations which assess ability not disability.

This example may be accessed from the website at www.welshdyslexia.info/dystrain/

The case study above has provided considerable information on how to ensure that good quality e-learning is achieved for all including the dyslexic individual. The tips below are not exhaustive, but give a brief insight into how others can help maximise learning for the dyslexic individual.

Ten Tips for Designers and Authors

1. Keep backgrounds clean and eliminate distracting items if they do not add to the learning.
2. Make navigation simple, consistent, easy to learn, use and remember.
3. Make the interface adaptable in colours (background and font) and fonts (type and size).
4. Ensure all components can be accessed by text-to-speech and other assistive technology.
5. For shared learning environments (e.g. chat areas and discussion forums), ensure dyslexia is not a restriction on participation.
6. Keep text width to less than 80 characters, sentences less than 20 words, use bullet points wherever appropriate and use left justified text.
7. Use methods, systems and conventions that are known to work with dyslexic individuals.
8. Ensure that the *dis*ability is supported, but it is *a*bility that is assessed.
9. Run trials with user groups.
10. Provide human support, both as a tutoring method, and for technical support.

Ten Tips for Users

1. Where the e-learning environment can be changed, change it to suit your needs.

2 Provide feedback to designers and content managers about the dyslexia friendly nature (or not!) of their website.
3 Where modifications to text cannot be made in the learning environment, see if it can be copied and pasted into another program such as Microsoft Word.
4 Talk to other users of the programme.
5 For chat and messaging, try composing in Microsoft Word (using their spellchecker) and then copying the message into the chat zone.
6 If the site is password protected, make sure the password is written down in several obvious places.
7 Make printouts wherever possible. These are often easier to annotate as well as less glaring than screens.
8 Use text-to-speech to access the content, if necessary copying the text into another environment.
9 If it does not work, do not assume that it is only you that has the problem.
10 Do not assume that everything has to be done using the computer.

A more in-depth analysis of these issues may be found in *Dyslexia and E-learning – a guide to good practice* by Ian Smythe and E.A. Draffan (2004) in Smythe, I. (Ed) (2004) *Provision and use of ICT by Dyslexic Students at University in Europe*. www.welshdyslexia.info/minerva

References

Supporting students with dyslexia in the effective use of C&IT in their academic studies (Accessed June 2004) www.edgehill.ac.uk/tld/research/sedafinalreport.pdf

A Dyslexic Perspective on e-Content Accessibility http://techdis.ac.uk/seven/papers/dyslexia-index.html

Concise, SCANNABLE, and Objective: How to Write for the Web http://www.useit.com/papers/webwriting/

Some additional hints from The Plain English Campaign Web: www.plainenglish.co.uk

Designing More Usable Web Sites http://trace.wisc.edu/world/web/index.html

Web Accessibility Initiative http://www.w3.org/WAI/about.html

You may also like to look at the BDA Dyslexia Style Guide at www.bda-dyslexia.org.uk/main/information/extras/x09frend.asp

Index of Advertisers

BDA Structure

The BDA & its Partners

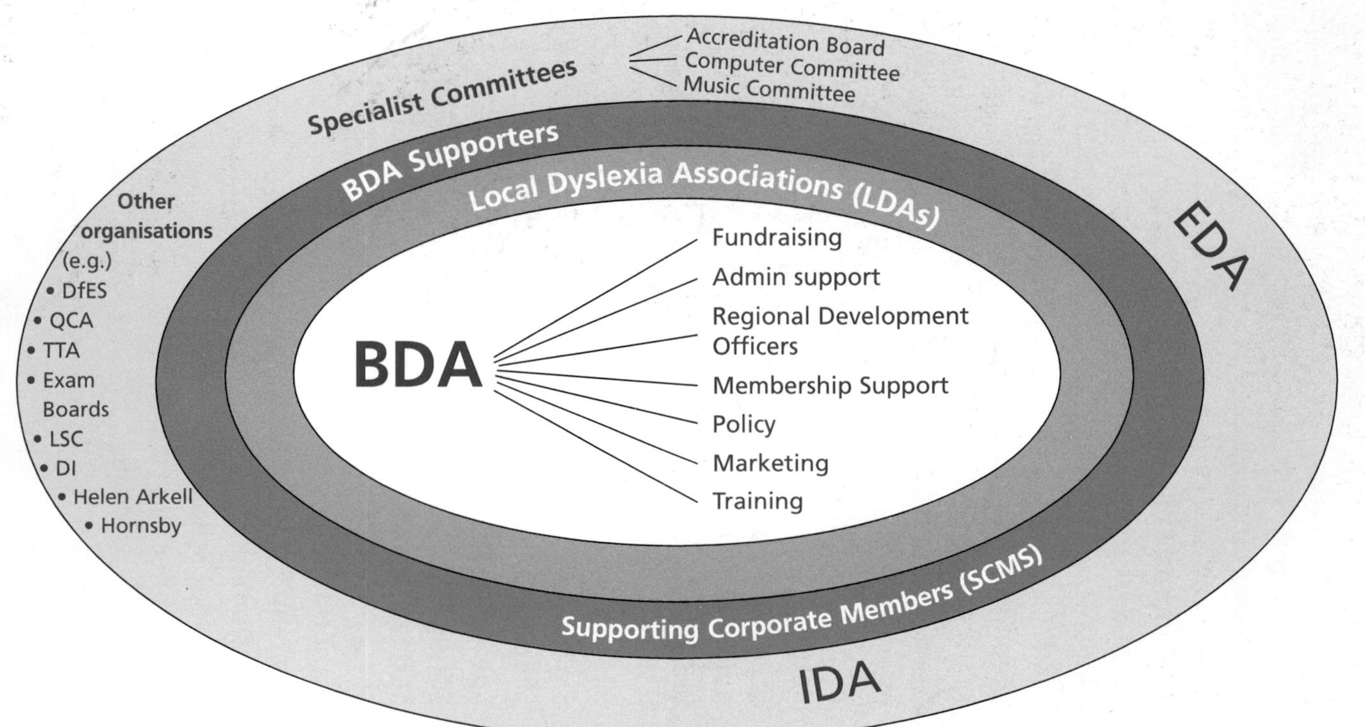